Quiet Voice, Awesome Power

Quiet Voice, Awesome Power

Connect with Spirit, Enlist Divine Help,
and Live Your Most Potent Life

Amanda R. Edwards

APOLLO
PUBLISHERS

Quiet Voice, Awesome Power:

Connect with Spirit, Enlist Divine Help, and Live Your Most Potent Life

Copyright © 2023 by Amanda R. Edwards

Visit our website at www.apollopublishers.com.

Published in compliance with California's Proposition 65.

Library of Congress Control Number: 2022950413

Print ISBN: 978-1-954641-24-2

Ebook ISBN: 978-1-954641-25-9

Printed in the United States of America.

Contents

To Pa
for showing me the alternate routes

and to Mom
for showing me the faith for the road.

Introduction

Spirit Is You

I am so excited you're here to dive into the power of spirit with me. To be real with you right from the start, though, I have to admit that this book makes me a little uncomfortable. For one thing, I'm writing about a loaded subject, a topic much of the world believes is solely the purview of religions and much of the rest sees as frivolous or imaginary. On a more personal level, with this book I'm effectively shining a spotlight on a path whose shadows I've been accustomed to walking in for most of my life. Even as a mystic, or spirit medium, who has worked with clients for many years, I've let word of mouth among them grow my practice rather than loudly calling attention to it. Did I also mention a book is made up of a lot of words, and so many moments of spiritual significance transcend words?

But here we are: me, despite my discomfort, choosing to light up this subject that gives both immense well-being and purpose, and you, choosing to tread with curiosity and take a path away from those who'd rather rest in their certainty. You're here to wonder and ask questions about spirit for yourself rather than take anyone else's word for it (including mine, I hope). And I hope it all makes you just a little uncomfortable too. Adventures into new possibilities have that effect, but I can promise you're not alone on your journey.

I wasn't always so confident in the choice to pursue a spiritual journey off the beaten path. I grew up as a typical American material girl living in a material world. (I never dressed like Madonna, but I definitely tried my best in elementary school to dance like her.) My family had a spiritual tradition that included church on Sundays and daily prayers before dinner and bedtime. But the secret prayers of my heart and my conversations with what I instinctively felt were my own version of God in a multiplicity of forms and emissaries—including an uncommon brand of ghosts outside my bedroom window and at the foot of my bed—stayed hidden and quiet. There was no legitimate place in the world I knew then for the work that I do now and the person I became doing it.

Eventually, my ability to sense spirit in everyday situations would not quiet down anymore, showing up like a code of symptoms, signs, and synchronicities I couldn't ignore. Without the cultural or community support of mentors or peers to help me interpret the code, I embarked desperately on an independent study of sorts. Over a few years of tumultuous life events, which, it turns out, are remarkable practice ground for strengthening a spirit connection, I met new people who experienced spirit like I do, and soon I found the confidence to use and speak to a few others about those gifts I'd kept silent.

Spirit in the Muck

One of the hardest things to learn (and to teach) about cultivating a connection with spirit is that in this unique relationship, you get the biggest nourishment and most startling gifts from it by not paying direct attention to it. We're used to thinking we need to force, cajole, or manipulate into place the things we care about most, but both the subtly powerful and the socks-knocking-off encounters with spirit require us to focus our energy elsewhere. Just as we can't actively make a flower grow out of soil, we don't make our connection with divine energy happen with force. Instead, like all the microscopic participants in the ground contributing to that eventual blossom, our job is to adhere faithfully to the truest version of ourselves and let life-force energy flow natural miracles through us the same way. That's what I've come to understand those moments to be when spirit has shown itself most resplendently to me. Each time, I've happened to be immersed, enthralled, caught up, or entangled in the most intense living that my life has ever demanded of me. In other words, the divine has appeared powerfully within the muck, my ugliest messes, sometimes in a spirit form I never could have imagined, much less conjured by force of will.

I often say my story of fostering close contact with spirit should start in the middle, with a world-shattering encounter I had that helped me make sense of countless earlier experiences then launched me forward to use my gifts openly. The state of my life at the time certainly qualified as muck. I was taking painful steps to leave a marriage, effectively blowing up my life (a phrase borrowed from my mentor and former therapist Rick, whom you'll get to know in Chapter 7, which he uses to describe a long-ago period of his own disruptive choices that stunned, hurt, and dismantled his family, career, and community). I'd had a seemingly great life after starting a beautiful family with my college sweetheart, but I'd silently felt a bewildering disconnect from the day I walked down the aisle into the utterly safe, small world we built together. After separating, I kept up all the logistics of raising my then slightly less perfect family, as many people had called us pre-split, while my body became systemically inflamed with chronic illness and my heart became consumed by a new and disastrous romance that was as far from safe and small as could be.

It was within that mess that I began to experience an unlikely and unrelenting allegiance—with a spirit. It started with an unforgettably vivid dream of a woman I somehow knew to be my new lover's mother, who had recently died without my having met her. From then on, she'd return in regular "conversations" during waking hours in which I could hear a voice entirely distinct from my own inner dialogue offering me specific insight, reassurance, or encouragement to move through the traumas I was facing almost daily in many of my relationships at the time. The troubling thing (besides seeing signs from and having regular chats with a ghost) was that I felt so certain of this friendship with a woman I'd never met, who'd died suddenly not long after I'd met her son, giving me no right or reason to have a bond with her other than our shared love for him. It seemed beyond crazy, and, in my world, impossible to tell anyone about it.

Thankfully, I could still count on my best friend in the living world to stick with me through "impossible," and we took a leap together to visit a spirit medium I'd found on Yelp. (That friend is my soul sister Cadence, whom I'll introduce more thoroughly in Chapter 3.) I've saved the recording I made of that head-spinning session so many years ago to remind myself of the miracle of hearing a stranger describe in complete detail aspects of my life including the spirit relationship I'd been hiding from the world in confusion for almost two years by that time. I've probably listened to it only once or twice. Now having been on the other side as deliverer of such messages for more than a decade since that day, I get to feel the power of that epiphany all over again with every one of my clients in spirit readings.

The point here of that story—which could fill volumes if I were to elaborate on that messy time in my life or speculate about why divine guidance took the singular, unbelievable form it did for me then—is to share that spirit guidance will come to you if you let it. Your job is not to live anyone's definition of a perfect life or to call loudly for a specific picture of the divine with precise prayers and rituals. It's to meet the path in front of you with the most authentic body-mind-spirit self you can become from moment to moment. Then learn to hear the quiet voice always encouraging you forward, whomever it sounds like.

Why I Think You're Really Here

A lot is different now than when I went hunting for answers about my mysterious ability to channel connection with a spirit all those years ago. Today the media and plenty of its popular personalities often talk about the idea of individual spiritual power, language from pop spirituality has made its way into everyday conversations, and movies and TV shows offer stories (mostly for entertainment over education) of people who hold strong psychic mediumship gifts. On social media I've observed countless accounts where people openly offer those gifts to help others—without any fear of a witch trial or straitjacket like the many (women especially) in the history of Western civilization who suffered that fate for their spiritual inclinations. All good progress.

But subtler forms of alarmism and social rejection still surround spirit communication. The natural human tendency to fear, avoid, or attack what we don't understand is what kept my most confounding but most useful natural gifts from living and breathing in the open for decades of my life. You felt drawn to open this book, so I suspect you have your own version of that natural gift inside and that yours is squirming to dance and sing too. And the thing about natural gifts is, they don't do so well with compartmentalization or rigid rules. They need fostering, the freedom of trial and error, and a nurturing community to help them along a path to good use.

Even with a greater prevalence of spiritual talk on the airwaves, there is little societal support for the strongly gifted intuitive person to unleash their gifts in an industrialized culture. There is no established scaffolding on which to hang life's big questions for examination and consultation. And if there is one inevitable feature of a journey with spirit, it is the continual appearance of big new questions. Yours may be about anything from "How can I know for sure that my beloved dad is still with me since he died?" to "Have I lived past lives as entirely different beings?" or "Is my soul's energy trying to sabotage my job and steer me toward a new purpose?" Maybe you've asked why you have a funny feeling someone is lying to you or whether you might be sensing a natural disaster is coming. Having a wide variety of questions about the nature of life and our reasons for living is quite common, but in most modern social structures, calling on the spirit aspect of ourselves to help answer them is not.

It's possible you came to this book for tips to communicate with the dead, and you'll get them. But I think your soul knows you're really here for even more. And you shouldn't hesitate to take more. Start with the expectation that unlocking a whole set of quiet capabilities might change your life more than you'd imagined.

A Beautifully Hopeful Choice to Dive into the Ocean of Spirit

Just as the sea holds power and mystery that we long to see and touch, even while knowing their enormity escapes us, the invisible details of the universe are vast, varied, and compelling. Many of its truths remain inaccessible to us if we are entirely absorbed with our material, physical existence, but we can learn how to participate in the expansive nature of the universe we come from and enjoy its generous wisdom by engaging the power of spirit. In truth, from the messages I receive, we are relearning our essential being in doing so, as our eternal souls never cease their participation in the universal life.

Before reading any further, take a moment to appreciate the gift of choice itself. In living your human life, you have the capacity to do with it whatever you imagine or desire because of the forces of nature we call free will and focus. In any circumstance you encounter, you employ those two abilities, and often without noticing you're doing so. By steering your will and focus more intentionally to connect and collaborate with spirit energy, you can accomplish an incredible array of feats that some people would consider superhuman or fictional but that are actually the natural gifts of our divine nature.

Whether you're beginning the journey of intentional connection with spirit for the first time or have already gone a long way down the path before picking up this book, I'm confident you will surprise yourself with beautiful new experiences as you absorb and use this material. Some confusion or frustration along your spiritual journey is natural, as it is not a linear process. But all the support you need to overcome challenging moments is available to you, both in spirit form and from other curious seekers. I can tell you with certainty, there are a lot of us.

Time for the Dive!

Our focus on this journey is the often invisible, seemingly intangible part of our being alive, which takes a degree of faith to understand and engage fully. But asking you to have faith in a process is not the same as telling you what to believe. My goal is to facilitate experience-based discovery that brings you right back to the physical, tangible parts of living. To this end, I will offer you suggestions and guidance but not assert any particular religious dogma or set of rules. And while I will share my story and those of a number of my clients and friends, I know from years of experience that you will be most transformed by what you see and feel for yourself.

As spiritual trends sweep through social media, with its emphasis on instant gratification and attention-grabbing drama that can cloud divine truths, I have realized a crucial component of my work is to take a genuinely pragmatic approach. You may have already discovered that flashy spiritual shortcuts, dressed-up ceremonies, hallucination experiences, or the adoption of others' spiritual traditions can be pretty hard to sustain in your own space, where you have your unique routines. But tuning in to your innate spiritual awareness does not require a total life overhaul. Whatever your path of seeking may lead you to try, I can promise the approach in this book will not require you to become someone new. Instead it aims to be of real value to the self you most naturally and deeply are already, with genuine, lasting empowerment.

What You Can Expect

The background and suggested "try this" practices in each chapter promote your own firsthand experiences. You will also find guidance and suggestions gleaned from my journey to develop my acute but initially messy ability to sense and communicate with spirit, and I provide an array of tips and tools from others I have encountered in my spirit work, reading, and everyday life. I aim to offer you a practical starting place to experience the topic of each chapter, plus as much variety of context as possible to support your discovery from there.

My approach favors radical inclusion. We humans are an incredibly diverse family with varied strengths and perspectives, and our spiritual power is the part of our nature that makes way for both yours and mine to shine through. Wherever possible, I describe an element of practice in more than one way. Where specific terminology or methods are helpful, I explain in those sections why I've made that choice of vocabulary, order of steps, and so on.

Your First Assignment, Should You Choose to Accept It

When I start introducing my spiritual approach to someone for the first time, I think of one incredibly gifted client I worked with in spiritual mentoring over many weeks. Starting out with a lot of energetic roadblocks from her repressive upbringing, she went through frustrations and doubts and sometimes looked at me funny when I presented an exercise for her to try. But like the steady drip of a faucet's water filling up a bucket, change was clearly underway in her, and one day it hit me suddenly that I was getting to see one of my favorite movie allegories unfold in real time. For as long as I can remember, movies like The Karate Kid, Rocky, and more recently Hustle have been films I can watch and rewatch without ever tiring of them. The unique gifts and complex background of the student mixing with the specific style and viewpoint of the teacher to create a powerful learning experience for both of them has always enthralled me. I've inhabited both roles at different points in my life, and my love for the dynamic makes me think I'll be a lifelong student no matter how long I've been a teacher.

While I used to think I was attracted to those movies because I love sports, I started to notice the scenes that most intrigued me all had something else in common. The mentor/teacher in every story demands the student carry out a mundane activity without much explanation (who can forget "Paint the fence . . . Sand the floor . . ." from The Karate Kid?), compelling the student to do it over and over again until the purpose of what at first seemed like an inane action becomes crystal clear as something more powerful.

Try to honor the many ways your complex body-mind-spirit apparatus learns as you progress through this book. The chapters intentionally build on each other with a holistic end goal in mind. The more fully you engage with all of a chapter's components from an attitude of curiosity and trust, the richer and more life-enhancing your relationship with your spiritual power can become. I can only invite you to find out for yourself as I have discovered, along with so many others I've had the thrill to connect with in spirit communication along the way.

So come join us—and the welcoming souls in spirit who guide us!

Terms and Definitions

Words have power—spirit energy!—so clarifying nuanced concepts through language has always been one of the most important and challenging parts of my work. We all give words our own distinct assignments, and examining those meanings is a valuable step for communicating about and with spirit. To share my approach and experience in spirit communication with you so that you ultimately become the author of your own approach, here is a bit about what I am referring to when I use the following terms:

Divine - The highest state and true essence of all life and creation, which is able to manifest in any form, including our human selves, for any life-affirming, life-generating purpose. Clearest to humans as unconditional love and reverence, the divine appears just as powerfully in the mundane, showing itself in the diverse complexity of nature, the perfect balance in music, creative expression, enterprise, and other awesomeness that resides in the everyday.

Spirit - The nonphysical, energetic life essence that permeates every person, place, and thing in the universe. Even concepts like numbers and aesthetic beauty have spirit energy.

Soul - A specific spiritual energy that takes the form of a human or animal but does not rely on a physical body to exist perpetually. Also the component of someone's being that holds and carries their divine purpose, whether living physically or non-physically.

Higher self - Also called the inner being, this refers to a person's soul-level viewpoint that intimately knows and operates as divine perspective through each of us. The higher self is always available, though sometimes ignored, muffled, or denied in the course of human experience.

Meditation - Any experience of releasing the active thought of the egoistic mind (our self-interested and self-protective viewpoint) to the extent that a person reaches a receptive state toward the higher self's divine perspective. It is possible to meditate in stillness and while the body is active.

Communing - The experience of intuitive awareness of other souls through a spiritual connection (distinct from communicating, which is an imparting of details through a participatory exchange). Meditation is one effective path to both communing and communicating with spirit.

Empath - A person who is keenly sensitive to emotions, physical feelings, and/or spiritual context in a situation. Though highly intuitive by nature, empaths may or may not have developed the skills to interpret the content they sense.

Psychic - Describes nonphysical means for picking up information and other phenomena of physically inexplicable awareness, whether about people or events. Every person has psychic ability, even without developing or acknowledging it.

Medium - Someone able to connect with souls who are not physically embodied. A highly psychic person does not necessarily have a strong gift for mediumship, but mediumship is a psychic ability.

Part I

Your Unique Human Apparatus

Part 1

1

First, the Body: Cultivate a Clean Machine

Remember learning about the five senses in kindergarten? And a few years later, studying those cross-sectional diagrams of the human body's anatomical parts? No matter how ethereal, lofty, or esoteric your encounters with spirit and the divine universe become from here on, I hope you'll always keep in mind your early, elementary awareness of your physical body. Yes, we will be talking spirit here most of all, but we will both begin and end with aspects of the physical, day-to-day experience of being a human. Without intentional care for the body as your primary (bio-miraculous!) tool, you cannot reach the levels of enlightened power we all have the potential to realize. And without honoring our bodies' starring role in the quality of the human experience, any place of enlightenment we may eventually reach cannot have the valuable grounded effects it is truly meant to nurture.

The human body is, indeed, a miracle machine. Along with all of its functions we learn about in school, which are a perfect intertwining of the mechanical, chemical, and biological truths found in all life on earth, the body also provides us with everything we need to connect with, receive, and translate information from spirit. Just as your brain interprets a lemon drop on your tongue as that very specific, detailed item without your having to see the candy, it can translate the presence of very specific spiritual information in your vicinity without your having to see its form or texture. The big difference is simply in the subtlety of spirit content. And what do you need to detect subtle, quiet information? A refined, clean, physical machine.

Quite honestly, I came about this understanding of the body's ability to translate spiritual content by accident. Not like stumbling upon well-documented information in a book—as I did recently when I read the details of how honeybees detect flowers by electric charge through the tiny hairs all over their bodies, an exquisite example of nature's mechanisms for subtle detection—but by a mishmash of my life's toughest events, years of serendipitous encounters, and firsthand, gobsmacking surprises that came together over decades. It was more like completing an enormous jigsaw puzzle by accident, over many years, without a guiding picture.

It is from my own living of it, from studying others, and from message after message spirit has delivered to me that I know this truth: the body is an integral participant in our ability to recognize and flow with spiritual information.

The Opposite of a Perfect Machine

When I was growing up, I had no idea how lucky I was to be healthy basically all the time. I never missed school, not just because my parents prioritized education over everything else but because I truly did not get sick. I never broke a bone besides one in my right pinkie finger (landing badly from the high bar on the playground), never had my tonsils or appendix out (wisdom teeth, yes, but dental crowding is hardly illness), and never threw up (except after one slumber party when I ate too many M&M's and one frat party when Brett Bartman introduced me to vodka shots). I was taller than every other girl in my class and most of the boys, and while I did have intense growing pains in my legs as I soared to my full height by middle school, with Scandinavian heritage and a dad who was 6'9", there wasn't any mystery or deep concern for that suffering. As a kid I never had a reason to worry about, or even be very conscious of, my body's normal, healthy functioning. However, when I was twenty-one, all of that changed.

Minor health problems started happening sporadically when I was in college and might have seemed unrelated to me forever if it weren't for my sister's boyfriend at the time being in medical school. He heard me complaining about tiny purple bruises I'd noticed on my limbs and started quizzing me about whether I'd ever had any of a list of other symptoms he remembered from textbooks and lectures. I had. Every one of them. Rashes in reaction to the sun, random severe fatigue, pain in my joints, my fingers and toes turning numb and white in the cold or even when I was nervous. I'd thought they were simply the result of little defects in my system, but these glitches had started to grow more painful and were even debilitating on some days. When these pains were taken as a whole, my then-future brother-in-law said they might indicate a larger problem.

Over a few weeks right before Christmas of my senior year of college, I had a lot of blood tests ordered by three different medical specialists, and I officially became a chronic patient. The doctors conferred over the phone and agreed on and reported an official diagnosis: I had systemic lupus erythematosus, known as SLE or just lupus, an autoimmune disease that meant my body, which I'd always taken for granted to be a smoothly operating machine, was turning against itself from the inside, system by system.

I'd had no reason to see it before, but the Western medical establishment sweeps up people like me into a lifelong cycle of being a patient if we let it. For at least fifteen years I traveled from one kind of specialist to another, lab to pharmacy, MRI to ultrasound machine, and sickbed to church prayer list. My experience was pretty unremarkable in the United States. More than 130 million Americans—almost half the population—live with at least one chronic illness, from hypertension and heart disease to a mental health disorder, obesity, or an autoimmune illness like mine. That figure grew by fifteen million over the first decade of the millennium, and it's projected that by 2050, 142 million adults over fifty will have at least one chronic illness.[1] Ahem. Does it bother you like it bothers me to know the National Institutes of Health in our scientifically advanced era are telling us that the majority of us can expect to be chronically ill for half our lives? Medical struggles aren't the fault of doctors and hospitals working to treat them, are they? So why would I suggest the medical system sweeps us up into becoming patients and staying that way?

As cynical as it may sound, physicians stay in business only as long as the population is unwell. So as altruistic as some may be, the energetic focus of their profession is toward identifying, analyzing, and talking about the illnesses, problems, and flaws in our bodies. To support and fuel the continually growing diagnoses, it's impossible to ignore what has become the most powerful engine of all in this machinery: pharmaceuticals. An entire nation's economy could operate on the amount of money flowing through the world's pharmaceutical sales. By 2026 the total global pharmaceutical market has been projected to reach 2.14 trillion US dollars.[2] That's a big

1 Ansah, John P., and Chi-tsun Chiu, "Projecting the chronic disease burden among the adult population in the United States using a multi-state population model," *Front Public Health*. Vol. 10, 2022, https://doi.org/10.3389%2Ffpubh.2022.1082183.
2 Pharmaceuticals Global Market Report 2022, The Business Research Company, March 2022, https://www.reportlinker.com/p06241981/Pharmaceuticals-Global-Market-Report.html?utm_source=GNW.

number. How does it hit you to know that this is about the same size as the entire economy (Gross Domestic Product) of Canada in 2022? And of Russia?[3] It's no surprise that every other TV or internet ad seems to be for a new medication to help alleviate a problem you may never have heard of but that you start to wonder whether you need. And that long list of side effects every one of those commercials speeds through for legal purposes at the end? As a (former) chronic patient, I'll attest to how front and center the side effects can become; some were so impairing that comparatively I started to think the original symptoms that had sent me to the doctor weren't so bad.

When I found myself squeezing a little life in between medical appointments and barely recognizing my own face in the mirror because of the medications I was on, these figures about pill sales and the nation's chronically ill were not on my mind. What did start to build was an instinct to examine and reform my own fundamental beliefs about my life and well-being. A quiet question kept whispering at me from within: "Could this glaring, perpetual unwellness really be what nature intends for you?"

A Major Ground-Level Shift

Why not ask the same about humanity as a whole: Are so many of us here in these miraculous bodies just so we'll get sick and stay sick? I have to acknowledge here a privilege in the quality of education I got, which instilled the fundamental scientific understanding to view what was going wrong in my body, as well as the tools to think critically about everything I read or heard from others (physicians, books, even statistics) about it. Ultimately, those two forces helped embolden my

3 Koop, Avery, "Top Heavy: Countries by Share of the Global Economy." Visualcapitalist. com, December 29, 2022, https://www.visualcapitalist.com/countries-by-share-of-global-economy/.

quiet instinct to opt out of a system that had me and millions like me joining the numbers of chronically unwell while generating a huge cash stream for others. The new choices I started to make because of that instinct were very real and practical changes—new ways of eating, new exercise habits, new practices of attending to ailments naturally when they came up—and I found I was beholding my body's functions with new fascination and embrace. My grounded, daily practices not only launched me toward a new relationship with my body, they became the material scaffolding supporting an entirely new life I was moving into, one with waves of mental and spiritual revelations coming my way.

It's not my role to claim or prove that my holistic approach to wellness cured me of lupus. But I have not taken any medications, seen any physician more than once every few years, or suffered from any lupus symptoms since my current physical and spiritual practices became my weekly routine. The larger point of sharing my own medical history is, of course, spiritual. That physical journey took me from living in torment inside a thoroughly medicated, restricted body in my twenties to becoming a fully healthy, integrated being who is up to participating in a purpose to its maximum depth, height, and breadth. It was, precisely, chronologically, as my body became cleaner, stronger, and more flexible that I also began to notice the powerful activation of spiritual experiences I'd almost forgotten I'd had in childhood. I couldn't ignore that confluence of factors in my work to prepare for spirit readings or in mentoring others. Each success on that journey has only confirmed the truth in this principle: cultivating a clean and healthy physical machine is vital to your ability to bring valuable spiritual content into your real, lived experience.

Getting Practical: The Elements for Cultivating Your Own Clean Machine

KNOWLEDGE. At the root of an empowered relationship with your body is a foundational knowledge of the science behind how it operates. Among the flaws in keeping our innate spirituality and centuries of scientific discovery about life separate is that it seems to require us to choose sides. In the sound bite marketplace, you're either pro-science or spiritual; a rational atheist or unintelligently religious. How absurd to discount complex, powerful experiences of transcendence by falsely putting them at odds with the natural laws that govern life. On the flip side of that coin, we miss out on the full range of our spiritual tools if we presume to segregate from them our scientific knowledge of physics, biochemistry, or genetics.

Understanding and therefore being able to visualize the body's makeup becomes an invaluable spark of activation of the body as a spiritual tool. I'm not a science teacher or a physician, but I do suggest that you equip yourself with concrete scientific information about yourself. Anything you might have missed in school about your body's ten major systems—skeletal, muscular, nervous, endocrine, digestive, respiratory, cardiovascular, urinary, lymphatic, reproductive—is well documented and diagrammed for study on the internet or in books available at your local library. Start with an understanding of what a reputable scientific source is (i.e. original, firsthand scholarly research produced by people with accredited degrees, that has been reviewed by their peers who also have degrees that required years of study, and that is accompanied by nice long bibliographies of sources), and give those your attention. Whether gaining knowledge about the mechanisms of your immune system like I needed to do to cope with lupus or learning about the physical effects of sustained stress or substances on your body, you'll become empowered by the abundant knowledge bank available from centuries of research. With a good science foundation behind you, you inform and support good choices in caring for the physical mechanism you arrived in, with plenty of room to discover what habits and practices work particularly well for your best functioning. Diet and exercise choices and habits are common topics that apply to all of us in a unique way but often get generalized or muddled in the media and our social circles by others' opinions and by flawed reasoning disguised as science. It's your responsibility to learn how best to care for your unique body, based on both solid information and firsthand awareness.

HEART AND BREATH. What was the important first sign of life when you were new in your mother's womb? Your sweet, tiny little heartbeat. And as you grew, it got stronger and louder, and you could feel it in different spots in your body as a pulse, reminding you constantly of your enduring viability through any experience. That heartbeat tells you when you're around someone who makes you nervous, scared, or deeply in love. It reliably offers such a message well before the words can form for you to think or say it. If you're not already taking a moment every day to notice the heart beat that is so critical to the way your body feels, be sure to add the habit to your routine somewhere between brushing your teeth and heading out for the day. After establishing that path of awareness in the morning, you'll be able to "give the heart a glance," something I teach in my mindfulness practice, at any point during the day to recenter your attention to originate from a vital, powerful place.

As soon as you direct your conscious mind toward your heartbeat, you'll notice something else closely related, that next critical sign that you were alive when you were born into the world: your breath. The pathway for oxygen, the essential element to all of life itself, the breath occurs without conscious effort, much like the heartbeat does. But the marvel of it is that your breath is also a constantly available instrument you can intentionally pick up with focus, altering its cadences, intensity, and direction. In practicing breathwork, just as you might practice playing a flute, you are honing your direct physical connection to the universal pathway of all life. It is no coincidence that the Latin root of "respiration" is *spirare*, meaning "to breathe," and from its noun form, *spiritus*, our word "spirit" came to mean the animating vital principle of all beings. As you explore your awareness of spirit in its many forms, you'll get to know your breath as a vector on which your spirit meets the spirits of others.

POSTURE. We all had someone—a mom, dance teacher, drill sergeant, or coach—tell us to "stand up straight!" at some point (or often) when we were growing up. In a lot of cases, that exhortation was about how the person wanted us to look on the outside, how we presented ourselves to the world. Other times it was about the way we carried our body, as that physical composure had a direct effect on how well we'd carry out a task they were teaching. Both points have valuable bearing in our bodily preparation for spirit awareness and connection too. Straight and centered posture is a simple, intentional way to present yourself spiritually and energetically for what you'd like to call toward you. Consciously planting yourself on the earth with intentional posture, whether seated, standing, or even fully prone, has a specific effect on how energy flows through you. Anyone who has practiced yoga or dance, or surfed, ridden a horse, shot a basketball, or swung a golf club (to name only a few examples) knows the body's precise positioning has this power. In the same way, your expertise in your body's alignment is enormously valuable preparation for sensing and translating information from spirit.

Does that mean you need to master challenging yoga poses to receive messages from a deceased loved one or dear friend across the globe? Certainly not, but that degree of physical training (in any athletic, dance, or martial arts pursuit) is an excellent opening to divine awareness. The yogic tradition specifically, with its emphasis on the balance of your physical body and your spiritual being, can be a powerfully transformative addition to your life with patient practice. But you can also enjoy noticeable positive changes in your perception, inner calm, and even bioregulation from simple small shifts to your posture. With better posture, not only does your breathing become easier and more effective, enabling the flow of life force through you, but your alertness and cognitive function may improve. In my workshops and spirit readings, I ask participants who may think they are just passive witnesses to adjust the quality of their posture for the sake of the quality of messages. Once they adjust their bodies I see an immediate change in the experience for all of us.

TRY THIS: Right now, wherever you're reading this, consciously straighten your spine and square your hips forward in line with the seat of your chair if you're seated, or in alignment with your shoulders and knees if you're standing. Elongate your neck, hold your chin parallel to the floor, and hang your arms loosely at your sides (this part may require you to scoot all the way to the front edge of your seat). Let the expression on your face settle into a neutral, relaxed position. Notice your breath. Notice your heartbeat. Visualize a straight, strong cord running all the way from the core of the earth through the top of your head. Acknowledge that your body is in perfect readiness for cooperation with spirit. (I suggest you try this posture alignment again throughout the day, and often; whether standing at the sink to wash dishes, reaching up to a shelf for a heavy object, or sitting in conversation with a dear person, give your posture a moment of awareness first and then adjust it into conscious alignment. As you proceed through the activity, appreciate how the preparation of your posture affects the flow of the experience.)

MOVEMENT. Just when you've gotten well rooted in a perfect, stationary posture, it's time to get yourself moving! (After all, there are plenty of opportunities to sit in stillness on your journey with spirit; personally, I'm a big fan of naps as a grounding tool.) Physical movement is far too important to your machinery to put it off for more than the occasional day of pure vegetating. In fact, if I had to identify one MVP in the array of tools necessary for connecting to your highest spiritual guidance, it would be this one. You might as well find this out now, early on, just like the students who sign up for one of my spiritual workshops and discover it'll include exercise. Friends who meet me for coffee often find out I have a walk-and-talk in mind, and my kids (like it or not) have had their Saturday lolling interrupted countless times by my insistence that we get outside and get moving. I'm a big advocate of motion for its myriad benefits beyond just physical fitness. It's not an exaggeration to say that every detail of my experience of the world changed for the better when I felt a new urge to begin running many miles every week. Just for starters, the habit triggered a more immediate awareness of my breath, heart rate, and posture, as well as the physics, biology, and chemistry of my body.

The exercise element of cultivating your body as a clean spiritual machine will do more to heighten your vivid, experience-based lessons in spirituality as a holistic endeavor than anything else can. That word "holistic" appears in a lot of contexts these days, from a spa treatment to a trendy preschool's advertised curriculum or even a government policy, so it's important to stop and appreciate that it means more than incorporating parts into a whole. Our goal is to come to know ourselves as whole body-mind-spirit humans, and in our steps toward connecting specifically with spirit, we take "holistic" to its furthest reaches of meaning by asserting that the body, mind, and spirit are inextricable, intertwined, and indivisible. One affects and is affected by each of the others, and their interactions become the whole "I" we come to know and love for its complex, wondrous nature.

I like the ways I've heard martial arts masters describe this human complexity as our tool for achieving the quality of life we want. Specific, repeated, and focused bodily movement is central to those traditions, not placed above or below our nature for thinking and feeling, but practiced as necessary for our best thoughts and feelings to come about. You've surely experienced that miracle of the solution to a problem popping into your mind while you're sweeping your patio, or a new idea for a project taking perfect shape while you're swimming. That's the same phenomenon that my spiritual colleagues and I have discovered boosts our connection to higher guidance. Your effective use of movement for spirit communication will not only draw upon aspects of the beautiful, ancient martial arts traditions, it will be activating the same essential mechanisms, under whatever traditional or nontraditional labels of language and approach suit you.

TRY THIS, PART A: Thankfully for the purposes of sharing them in this book, my go-to ways to use physical movement for clearing a pathway for spirit are pretty straightforward for almost anyone to make their own. The important factors are repetition (developing muscle memory) and attention to the minute details of your body's motions (refining your sensory keenness). I like to take a jog or do yoga at least every other day. Your regular exercise can be any mix of activities you enjoy that call for some amount of exertion. Pushing yourself a little—whether it's how much weight you can lift, how far or fast you can swim, how limber your muscles and joints can become—is equally as important as the care and precision of movement. For your spirit, the benefits happen seemingly magically alongside and interconnected with the boost that exercise gives your body's metabolism. You'll notice it's working by your heightened clarity, your energized sense of oneness with your surroundings, and your growing confidence in your personal power. If you decide those benefits will be the focus and goal of your exercise, even more than weight loss or a toned appearance, for at least thirty days, I'm confident you'll become more addicted and committed to exercising than you've ever been.

TRY THIS, PART B: You can help clear a pathway for spirit almost instantly in any moment by using slowly flowing and deliberate movements. In the minutes immediately before a spirit reading with a client, my preparation always includes motion. Even seated at a desk before a Zoom session, I simply engage my musculoskeletal system in whatever instinctive movements I feel like making, which might look from the outside a little like tai chi in a chair. I very literally and physically slip into the spirit energy flowing through the moment and become its conduit. During this practice, which I now do automatically without having to remind myself to include it, I know I'll begin to connect almost immediately to the spirit presence connected to the client I'm about to meet with.

For this movement, whether seated or standing, stretch your arms out to either side as if you're trying to touch the walls, but don't strain yourself. These motions, and physical exercise in general, are not more effective if they're painful. That isn't a sign that it's "working." What you want instead is for all your physical senses to attune with your spiritual ones. As you stretch your arms, feel the muscles along them engage and stir to life before next bringing your arms up over your head with your palms facing each other. As you move, gently notice the sensations throughout your body and breathe steadily. On an inhale, bring your arms down to create a round, open hug, as if holding an invisible beach ball. In that position close your eyes and add intentional breathing. Perhaps in rhythm with your breathing if that synchronization feels natural, let your arms respond to the energy between them (that invisible ball holds spirit too) by expanding outward to accommodate an enlarging, activated presence. Pause at a comfortable place with that energy held in your loose embrace before letting your arms open all the way and then fall back to your sides. You can stay here with your eyes closed and your palms facing forward for as long as you are relishing the spiritual content flowing through the moment. You can also keep motion going any way your body feels inspired to move.

(If that slow and silent approach doesn't do it for you some days, look up one of my favorite social media stars, Nicole Paris. An extraordinary beatboxer from St. Louis, Nicole seemingly cannot spit beats without moving her body in a joyful, coordinated flow. As you watch and listen to her, I challenge you to sit still. Then try to imagine whether she'd be able to make the same sounds if she were sitting perfectly still. That flow of positive energy through physical motion that results in heightened awareness, ability, and connection is what I call meditation in motion!)

Antonio's Story: The Power of Discipline

My friend and colleague Antonio Harrison intentionally engages his whole body-mind-spirit apparatus, and he does so with more discipline than anyone else I know. An expert in human behavior with a PhD in Behavior Analysis, Antonio was a talented athlete early on and says his awareness of spirit "began in physicality." Compelled to grow up fast while his father struggled with a crack addiction and was in and out of prison, Antonio found order and self-regulation as a young child in the practical, physical demands of everyday survival. Rising early to catch a school bus, protecting his little sister in their tough world, and keeping up with the physical training routines of his sports teams were daily habits that infused Antonio's formative years with perpetual motion. That is, until he was a college football star with plans for a professional athletic career and a severe injury halted him in his tracks. Antonio lived in a hip-to-toe cast for nine months as a college student, and it took a year and a half for him to start walking again. In that time he began to explore where else his personal identity and power might come from, and, reading voraciously, he began to light up from the wisdom of Zen Buddhism and other ancient philosophies that pointed toward empowerment rather than dogma. Naturally Antonio gravitated toward learning the exercise habits of spiritual masters, because to him their discipline and commitment clearly mirrored the qualities he'd learned make a successful athlete.

Fast-forward to Antonio's current life, in which he is thriving as a professor, fitness coach, husband, and father, and those early seeds of inspiration are obvious. I'd gathered for years that Antonio's personal wellness routine was pretty awesome in both consistency and rigor, but when he told me the specifics I realized I hadn't known the half of it. As much as I love the peace and stillness of dawn on occasion, I was a little gobsmacked to learn Antonio gets up every day, including on weekends, at 4 a.m. to ensure his whole being gets equal attention before his wife and kids are up and about. And he doesn't leave out the mental aspect of his development in forming intentional habits either. Along with daily exercise—boxing, swimming, or completing a routine he created from elements of Shaolin kung fu, one of the oldest forms of the martial art kung fu of Chinese Buddhism, and qigong, a Chinese system of coordinated movements, breathing, and meditation—Antonio reads sacred texts one excerpt at a time and reflects on their meaning in a journal.

Antonio's expertise in human behavior helped him identify the most important factor in anything he was going to make a conscious choice to do, from meditating to learning a new language: discipline. Antonio self-identifies as a consumer of a wide variety of source knowledge (he hunts down the teachings of the teacher of the teacher in whatever he's learning), and he always takes a scientist's approach of experimenting directly with that knowledge for himself. "That way, I fold these things into my life in ways I know they're actually beneficial," he explained to me. And those benefits? They're for his whole being in equal measure: "Yes, you can feel great on the inside emotionally, you can be completely spiritually aligned, but if your body's falling apart, you're not going to be here to share much with anybody. If you're way out in the spiritual realm without that physical ability to engage, what good does it do anyone?"

I had to notice the divine full-circle in Antonio's evolving relationship with spirit through the physical pathway of his relationship with his body. All the while enlisting a mindset he'd instinctively relied on as a child then as a young man to get through adversity, Antonio carved a holistic path of well-being we can all learn from.

ENVIRONMENT AND FEEDING. If you bought a brand-new car, all shiny and leathery smelling, with its inner mechanisms whirring in well-oiled synchronicity as it responds to your whims, would you park that car out under the neighborhood pigeons' favorite roost on the busiest street with gutters full of garbage and toss any old mix of fluids in its engine for maintenance? If this car example lacks meaning for you, choose whatever object or beloved being you treasure most—your heirloom watch, your child, pet, or nana—and consider how much care you put into ensuring the quality of surroundings, safeguarding, and nourishment for that dear item or loved one. Now consider the immeasurably complex apparatus of your human self in physical form that will carry you through this lifetime. That treasure deserves at least the same level of care and nurturing.

When I refer to your environment, I'm talking about both the energetic and the material quality of your surroundings, whether in temporary or longer-term living conditions. Materially, your environmental state might be something like, "I'm in a nature sanctuary nearly untouched by human hands," or, "I'm stuck in a dim and stuffy waiting room packed with people facing desperate times." Each extreme and the whole spectrum between holds certain spiritual energy that directly affects us. That energy also falls on parallel spectra between vibrational extremes that we can sense—balance and imbalance, equilibrium and chaos, heavy density and light openness. For anyone like me who's always had high sensitivity to energy, we got early lessons in the nuances of environments. As a kid I remember begging friends to go outside with me instead of playing in a closed, air-conditioned room for hours; as an adult I've left events suddenly many times, simply because the energy of the place or people felt excruciating to me. Now that I've been working with spirit for so long, I understand that a clear pathway for divine spiritual communication happens most naturally in a place of relative balance and higher vibration. Surroundings full of plant life and trees, water, and animals freely enjoying their habitat are the easiest places to feel and observe those qualities vividly.

Along with the kind of surroundings you find (or put) yourself in, it's important to be intentional about what you put into your body. Feeding our bodies entails food itself but also what we use to hydrate, any medicine or ingestible substances (including things we inhale), and even what we apply to our skin. I'll say it again and again: our physical bodies are miraculous tools that deserve the best care. Is our food straight from nature or highly processed and engineered? Are we taking substances that alter our brain function, metabolism, or cardiovascular function, or do we choose the most purely sustaining and boosting nourishment available? Just as an environment has an energy, the things we put into our bodies hold energy. The cleaner, naturally balanced, higher vibration choices (food, drink, and medicine that's closer to the earth's natural sources and processes) best support your body's readiness for divine spiritual connection.

So without any of the societal judgment about diet and the ways that what you eat can affect how you look, try thinking about the way you feed yourself as a spiritual act. The goal of cultivating your clean machine for spiritual power is to join your physical being with the earth's natural cycles of providing. How marvelous that we can not only survive but thrive on what grows around us! Studies of the world's healthiest diets continually show that making effective use of what is abundant and accessible within a population's own geographical area has positive effects on longevity and wellness. Those mindful, practical (not to mention environmentally friendly) habits help to align the body as a clean and receptive vessel for divine spirit. As soon as my life put me face-to-face with my ability to communicate with the spirits of people who'd died, some of the most distinct physical changes I noticed were sudden cravings for healthier, plant-based meals and simultaneous aversions to meat, dairy products, heavy fried food, and other substances my body told me it did not need.

Whether a food or substance has a cleansing or toxifying effect can be easy to determine in some cases, but there are plenty of things we can consume that fall into a grayer area. Some ingestibles carry mixed messages from the medical field, our parents, or social media. After decades of experimenting and exploring the nuances of my results compared to those of others, I'm convinced we need to learn and know our own bodies and what they are asking to be fed and to take others' endorsements as secondary input. The reaction your apparatus has to ingesting certain things won't be the same as it is for a friend or even a genetic relative, so blindly adopting another person's regimen, cure-all substance, or secret diet trick never makes great sense.

Not only are we all wired uniquely on a physical level, we have different purposes that drive us, so I don't prescribe specific boundaries everyone must set or checklists we should consult for an environment or a dietary plan to pass spiritual muster. Working with individual clients, I am more apt to help identify those specifics based on their unique spiritual and energetic makeup, and my recommendations can vary widely. However, we can all use certain guiding principles to help us make good choices for our own holistic body-mind-spirit apparatus. First, revisit the element of knowledge and remember how valuable a basic scientific understanding of the body is to being able to discern whether an environment you put yourself into supports your machine's well-being or not. Understanding the fundamental workings of the human psyche holds the same value. Abundant scientific research explains the ways toxic psychological or emotional environments affect us, and particularly when we have keen sensitivity to energy, their traumatic effects can be as physically detrimental as smog in the air or chemical additives in food.

The more fine-tuned to spirit energy you are, whether it's part of your nature or you're getting there through intentional practice, the likelier you are to find that the quality of your environment and what you ingest affect you in extreme ways. Those reactions can be noticeable as any strange physical symptoms, like a rash or digestive upset, or as symptoms pertaining to your mental health, like your level of clarity or anxiety. It is very important to consult with licensed medical professionals for health concerns you have; at the same time, I hope you'll feel assured knowing that a natural and balanced approach to incorporating more spiritual awareness into your life can only add health benefits over time. The more powerful way to frame that claim is to emphasize the flip side: your body-mind-spirit apparatus is always asking—with a quiet voice like a craving or louder messages like symptoms and signs—for an environment and nourishment that will support wellness. Read my client Clara's story for her beautiful example, which was guided by spirit messages. This part of caring for yourself does not need to be a mystery; you'll know when you're getting what you need from clean air, the vitamins and minerals that nature offers in their purest forms, and uplifting environments that you choose to immerse yourself in.

Clara's Story: The Power of Environment

One client I've seen in spirit readings had a series of memorable encounters that shone a light for her—and for me—on the simple abundance of nature's solutions for our physical well-being. When someone comes to me for a session, I intentionally avoid asking them any questions. I've learned that no matter how self-aware we are, the human spin on a story tends to cloud the direct and supportive messages spirit can offer, so I go straight to an energetic connection to provide me the context for what each person needs most.

At the start of one visit with Clara, I was aware of the presence of her paternal grandmother looking toward her with an especially bright, love-filled nature. When I told this to Clara, she scowled and said that the woman who'd raised her father had not been bright and love-filled in her memory. The presence persisted joyfully, though, and as I shared more details like seeing her grandmother in the South and dressed for hard work in an apron, Clara realized they matched her true grandmother—the mother her father had lost when he was very young before a new stepmother arrived and raised him. Sure enough, as we continued, the signs of confirmation became even stronger for me that Clara had hooked in with the right person. She didn't need to have known this grandmother during her lifetime for there to be a strong spiritual bond between them. And indeed, the messages this woman had for Clara about her physical health proved the connection was also quite practical.

I picked up image after image of saltwater from Clara's grandmother. At the start of the session, I was shown gentle ocean waves offering an obvious reference to saltwater, and as we "spoke" in our inaudible language, I understood the woman wanted Clara to swim in it, bathe in it—in any way submerge herself in water—but very specifically it was to be saltwater. Clara, for her part, shared that she had a strong personal connection to the ocean and loved to visit the beach but that she hadn't gone for a swim in some time. During the reading I also picked up tingling sensations in my arms and a sudden feeling of weakness in my body, so I asked Clara if she'd been having trouble with her limbs. She confirmed that she had and, in fact, was struggling with nerve and circulation problems that severely affected her use of her arms and legs. She was scheduled to have a heart procedure the next day for her doctor to investigate the issue further.

After the reading session, I received a series of exhilarated texts from Clara. She had uncovered some details and couldn't wait to share them. Her dad had told her that his birth mother had lived and worked in Hot Springs, Arkansas, renowned for its four-thousand-year-old natural springs. Clara's grandmother had worked for years at one of the national park's public baths where people came to soak in the water for its healing benefits. She sent me a screenshot of an article, "The Medicinal Value of the Various Salts and Gases Present in the Mineral Waters," about Hot Springs. All the more soul-stirring, Clara told me, was extensive research she'd found that demonstrated the benefits of Epsom salt baths on cardiovascular health. Her grandmother had not only led Clara to new knowledge about her body and nudged her toward a healing environment she could immerse herself in any time but she had also brought her a new sense of elation about the promise of getting well.

Over the weeks that followed, Clara sent me photos of more signs. One day she was unpacking from a move and found a gift she'd forgotten a friend had sent her. It was a basket containing a set of cards titled "Heal Thyself" along with—what else?—bath salts. More recently, she was in a thrift store and found a whole shelf of brand-new candles with the label "Sea Salt Bergamot." A new reminder of well-being in the Goodwill store, and a new relationship with a grandmother she'd never known.

2

Next, Your Mind: Beliefs Matter

There's no denying that what we believe affects what we do and experience in our day-to-day lives. A belief is a consistently held thought about what is true, what exists (and many actions spring from our thoughts, conscious and subconscious). If we believe generally positive things about ourselves and what we have to offer the world, we apply for the job, make a move toward the cute girl, and speak up for our rights. If we believe nature is not an exploitable resource but an integral part of our existence, we keep our trash off the hiking trail, catch the cricket in the kitchen to release it outside, and avoid buying single-use plastic. Neuroscience even tells us that our unconscious actions, not just breathing and walking but awesome, complex things people seem to do reflexively—like LeBron James performing a spin dunk or Arthur Rubinstein playing a Brahms piano concerto by heart—owe thanks to the brain's incredibly useful automation mechanisms. The more an action is practiced, including repeated conscious thought, the more the brain takes over the work and ensures it happens automatically.

Our relationship with spirit, as you'll discover for yourself through practice, is not unlike the art of the slam dunk or the art of the musical intermezzo. There are elements of the ability to connect with spirit that appear naturally strong in some people, just like an athletic gift or musical ear, and just like strength in sports and music, interaction with spirit becomes real through desire and conscious practice. At the foundation of what you'll be practicing is your set of beliefs. If LeBron didn't first believe he could jump over another player, spin around midair, and still make the shot, it would never happen for him to enjoy and for us to witness and believe too.

In our early years, many of our teachers don't trust us to reach our own profound conclusions, so they drill their beliefs into us. Later, institutions push certain beliefs to maintain the status quo or achieve power by compelling mass behavior. Even in our personal relationships, we favor people who believe what we do, because it feels safe and reassuring (even when our shared belief makes us both miserable). The number and volume of voices telling each other what to believe has leapt exponentially with the digital media age. "Influencer" is an immediately recognizable (and to many a perfectly legitimate) job title. In that soup of continuous campaigning for mental and emotional loyalty, it's no wonder if you've noticed yourself covering your ears and trying to avoid believing anything at all!

As understandable as the shunning of beliefs on your body-mind-spirit journey may be, doing so is just as problematic as a blind willingness to believe anything. Both approaches, while seemingly opposite, share a common lack of a solid mental floor for your spirit to work from as you engage the diverse world you encounter. Blindly believing anything keeps you in a tenuous, easily swayed condition of weakness. Stubbornly believing nothing leaves you without a portable home base, the reliable launching pad from which to move confidently from each new experience to the next. So from both a practical standpoint and a visionary one, belief matters.

The challenge to you in this second step on a journey of empowering spirit connection will be to explore the middle ground where you may need to reevaluate unhelpful beliefs you've been carrying on the one hand and stretch past any automatic disbelief on the other. Considering how fixated our culture is on the material content of life, nurturing and embracing an open, wide-eyed wonder at out-of-this-world truths can be the hardest part of spirit connection for many seekers.

Is Traditional Religion the Problem?

To enjoy our most empowering connection with spirit, it's important that we not confuse or conflate spirituality and religion. Each has enough of its own vastly different iterations to generate confusion, which can lead many people to regard the whole baffling lot with suspicion. One of my favorite memoirists, Mary Karr, wrote, "The American religion—so far as there is one anymore—seems to be doubt. Whoever believes the least wins, because he'll never be found wrong."[4] Some subscribers to the religion of doubt like to loudly publicize for all to hear that religion and spirituality are the same load of invisible hooey. (Ironically, they miss the fact that their own adamant certainty is the flip side of the same coin.) Instead of mixing up or dismissing religion while we explore spirituality, I find it's a useful exercise with my clients and students to acknowledge their points of similarity and the places they diverge.

---

4 Karr, Mary, *The Art of Memoir* (New York: HarperCollins Publishers, 2015), 89.

In particular as we proceed through specific suggestions for intentionally engaging with spirit, you'll run across elements that might seem to echo aspects of religion you've either embraced or avoided in the past. Sitting in meditation to connect with spirit might seem a lot like sitting in prayer in a house of worship, for example, and if that comparison strikes a triggering chord for you, it's actually a helpful problem spot. Instead of letting, say, the discomfort you had as a child in a rigid church cause you to miss the valuable benefits of a relationship with spirit now, let it tell you something useful about the effect of a particular religion on your beliefs and experience. If, on the other hand, you find yourself filling your meditations with imploring prayer because that's how you were raised to believe the divine will respond, it signals you're accustomed to specific religious practice shaping your experience with spirit.

The topic of belief marks an important fork in the road where, for the purposes of the spiritual journey I invite you to take, we'll depart from religion—not because I don't value it in many forms (I do), but because I believe it will offer you clarity about your pure and natural-born gift to communicate with spirit, independent of man-made, society-reflecting structures. Organized religion is, at its basic—and potentially positive—foundation, our human system for sharing spiritual experience and beliefs in community with others. We're herd animals. We thrive on that communal sharing.

In the simple, early forms of religions, they provided texts, rituals, and routines designed to teach and reaffirm whatever the inspired or contrived beliefs of their founders were. We cannot say across the board whether religious belief is good, bad, cuckoo, logical, or true; tenets of religion are far too many, too varied, and too susceptible to (often misinformed) outside opinions for broad characterization to be possible. What we can generalize about them is that in the act of organizing, religions began to carry a mission to spread their specific beliefs across many people and generations. Religious structures gain obvious benefit in promoting a belief that winning more believers will bring great reward to the best belief spreaders. A promise of a seat in the fancy section of heaven, the personal approval of the community, or plain-old hard cash to funnel back into the belief-spreading business becomes part of a reward system that muddles natural, personal access to spirit. In too many cases, the bartering or monetizing of belief turns what could otherwise be a beautiful, uplifting, and fortifying spiritual experience into a compulsory, manipulative, or even oppressive power structure.

Does that mean healthy spirituality and communal religious practice can't go together? Absolutely not. Instead of jumping on a popular bandwagon that condemns any religion as an evil influence in the world (which I, who have drawn enormous spiritual knowledge and comfort from religious practices, could never do), we can for the purposes of growing a healthy direct relationship with spirit at least acknowledge the slippery slope of any path that requires people to tell each other what to believe. If you're among the younger readers of this book, I'll venture to say you're part of a generation better fortified from within to avoid those slippery slopes. The more each successive generation progresses toward celebrating individual autonomy and self-determination over groupthink, the faster obligatory participation and authoritative dogma lose loyal audiences.

And Then There's the Opposite Effect

Young or old, when we reject participation in any formalized, long-established belief structure, we're very much on our own to make our way through life's choppy waters with makeshift tools. This ad hoc, uncharted approach can be a fantastic adventure to undertake if you choose it, but for most people, a mix of adventure and the security of established knowledge is best; and the same can be said for our beliefs if we want to explore where a direct connection to spirit can take us. Knowing we hold a few fundamental beliefs that support us through periods of confusion can mean the difference between a tumultuous life and positive thriving.

I often get requests for guidance from deeply sensitive and intuitive people who find themselves in a swirling chaos of anxiety, life drama, or a major medical crisis. Many are in the early stages of adult responsibilities and freedom, with all the unsettling changes that transition brings, when a moment of spirit recognition lights them up with hope for a whole fantastical world of solutions they've always wanted. It can be a beautiful and heady time, even while life is crumbling all around us, to catch what feel like our first glimpses of the greater universe communicating right to us. I know, because my own period of awakening to spirit connection was an exhilarating disaster too.

Hannah's Story: The Power of Questioning

One college-age client of mine, Hannah, came for a spirit session as a gift from her mom. Since I don't exchange any personal details with people before readings, I didn't know that Hannah's mom had some substantial worries about her daughter's mental state and hoped for a new way to help her. What came through most strongly in the spirit messages I received was Hannah's own shining ability to intuit details of others' emotional worlds and convey them artistically. When I shared this awareness with her, she lit up at hearing herself described so accurately and in such a positive light. That's just the MO of our highest spiritual awareness—to reflect the most divine nature in everyone back to us, no matter how dormant it may be at the time. By far the best way my life has changed over the decade-plus that I've actively served as a spirit medium to others is the permanent hold that divine perspective has taken in my everyday consciousness. I have the lucky chance to hear and see it about everyone and everything because connecting with divine spirit so frequently has made it a fixed habit. Each one of us has the same opportunity to gain that perspective and have it last, but most people also have a whole heap of conflicting beliefs that choke off those senses and obscure that authentically rosy picture. Hannah, like many of us have, went through a period of pretty scary disconnection from any positive viewpoints of herself and the world.

"Having intrusive thoughts about suicide is very different from being suicidal," Hannah explained about her specific painful experience with obsessive compulsive disorder, or OCD. "You specifically don't want to die." Everybody has weird, dark, disturbing, or creepy thoughts. Somebody who doesn't have OCD can have a thought like that and not think it means anything about them. But someone with OCD, like Hannah, will have that thought and immediately think, *Well, what does that mean about me? Why would I have a dark thought if I'm not a dark person?* Those looping, cataclysmic thoughts gain free rein in the mind if there isn't a more powerful thought to interrupt or squash the loop.

Just as it became clear to Hannah that she'd have to drop out of school because of the total takeover of her negative thoughts on her life (she told me, "I remember trying to drive to school and thinking, How am I going to get there without driving my car off this road?"), she, thankfully, had a serendipitous moment when she heard an ad for a therapist on the radio. The questions in the ad spot sounded like they were meant for her, and soon she started sessions with that very specialist in OCD and learned some new belief statements that helped her gain an advantage and throw a wrench in her looped thinking. For example, the simple yet strong belief that "I am far more than any single thought I have" renders even compulsive thinking much less potent. It also opens the door for valuable introspection and wonder about the specific body-mind-spirit apparatus that "I am" truly is.

As Hannah described her journey to me, I realized she was learning through therapy and creating art to shift her belief orientation to the generously positive way the divine sees her—and all of us. If only every young person could find access to the serendipitous voice to lead them there!

So What Does Belief Have to Do with Spirit Connection?

If I'm going to keep asserting that it's not my (or any spiritual mentor's) role to tell another person what to believe, what are we doing here in a chapter claiming "beliefs matter"? Understanding that spirit flows in, around, and through everyone and everything in nature, wouldn't that mean we all get to connect with spirit naturally no matter what we believe?

Well, yes. But the quality and value of the spirit connection will vary dramatically with the quality and alignment (or misalignment) of your beliefs.

When I see a client in a spirit session or I lead a workshop, or even when I talk politics with my brother-in-law, I ask a lot of questions about how the other person or people arrived at a belief they've expressed, either directly or unwittingly, because the quality and depth of beliefs do matter (my family can tell you that there are times and topics on which I fire off those questions more emphatically than I need to). And contrary to what many of us like to think about our ability to show the world only what we want them to know, our strongest beliefs actually come across silently and powerfully enough to be understood without our saying them aloud. If you've been at all tuned in to popular spiritual speakers and writers during the last few decades, you've heard anyone from Oprah Winfrey to Paulo Coelho or Miguel Ruiz avow their version of "You are what you believe." As in, beliefs are so powerful as to become realized as your lived experiences. I have to concur from firsthand observation, both in my life and in those I read spiritually. So wouldn't it serve us to become extra discerning about which beliefs we embrace or release?

Melissa's Story: The Power of Association

My client Melissa, for whom I've done multiple spirit reading sessions and who has taken a couple of my longer workshops, asked me not long ago to help her figure out if she's "doing Reiki right." We had already worked together for years, reconnecting her to her spiritual nature, which at the time we met had become muted and muddled as a result of deep traumas and pain she'd experienced. Melissa had recently followed an intuitive lead to learn to practice Reiki, a healing art going back about one hundred years that has proven effective for bodily and spiritual wellness. She is an actor and lifelong dancer, and she teaches movement classes to people with neurological challenges like Parkinson's disease, multiple sclerosis, and traumatic brain injury or who are navigating the effects of a stroke. Melissa's awareness of the physical body, its capabilities, and its range of emotional states—and potential injuries—is incredibly keen.

When Melissa reached out to me for help getting Reiki "right," she had finished the two levels of training and energy attunement with a Reiki master that the tradition teaches readies one to begin practicing on others in person and at a distance. A few times Melissa had tried giving a healing session to her mom or a friend who was a willing guinea pig, and each time she didn't think much had happened—for them or for her. After decades of accomplishing artistic feats with her body, Melissa found it incredibly frustrating that this practice eluded her.

Could I offer any help as an outside observer who hadn't even actually observed her Reiki sessions, talked to the people she'd practiced on, or seen her Reiki master's approach to teaching? I'd been through Reiki certification myself and used it regularly with my clients, so Melissa was hoping I'd help by telling her precisely how I conduct my sessions, how I hold my hands, what prayers I use, and what sequence of gestures I make. I humored her and described in as much detail as I could how I prepare myself and the room, move my hands, speak, use a pendulum, and breathe as I practice Reiki on another person. "But I do every session a little differently," I had to tell her honestly, which I could see was a little exasperating for someone hoping for a magic button that would make Reiki useful for her.

Silently reminding myself of what I know matters most at the root of anything we do, I said, "Let's forget what my sessions look like, and I'm going to ask you a string of questions now, instead. First, what do you believe Reiki is?"

She looked confused, as if wondering, Doesn't she know that one already?

I asked again, specifying that I didn't want a definition but something more personal about what she thinks is happening in a successful Reiki session. And next, what made her want to learn to use Reiki in the first place?

At first, her answers were pretty dry descriptions of things others had said to her: "This is what I've heard Reiki is," "A lot of people have told me I have healing hands and should try it," "My Pilates clients ask me for recommendations to heal their injuries." Her frustration—and my mental aerobics—was intensifying with each dead-end answer. That is, until I heard her say something important: "I don't worry about any of this stuff when I teach my movement and dance classes. I just step into the room at the assisted-living facility, and it makes everyone so happy. I love that."

I paused with my eyes closed and decided to stop asking her what she believes about Reiki and take another angle.

"What do you think it is that makes those students so happy the second you walk in the room?" I asked.

"I just give something off that makes them feel good and forget their pain," she said, her gaze turning to a scene happening somewhere else. "But I'm not really different from anyone else. . . . I just show up, and it lifts their spirits."

"Do you really believe that? Do you think your racist neighbor or grumpy customers at a restaurant could walk in and make the elderly students happy?" I pushed. "What do you actually believe that 'something' is that you give off? It's invisible, isn't it? But you know it's powerful."

"Love, isn't it?" Melissa asked with a small smile.

"Love," I agreed and smiled bigger. "You love your students and they feel it. We're talking about that exact same 'something' when we ask for divine energy to flow through us to the person on the Reiki table."

Melissa's beliefs mattered most. The quiet voice she carried inside her in every moment that had opinions about the Reiki practice itself, about her abilities and purpose in doing it, about the nature of spirit energy, and about the human body and its injuries had power, and the power of each belief she held had created complicated scaffolding that set boundaries on how effectively she was able to conduct the healing sessions. And Melissa could feel something was off in her early attempts as she stumbled over those boundaries. Soon after our talk, her real experience as a Reiki healer shifted as she'd been hoping it would when she let this simple belief about herself take center stage: "I naturally flow love to others."

What About Wise, Seasoned Teachers?

If you've had good teachers in any subject, from clarinet lessons to driver's ed to advanced calculus, you know they are immensely valuable. And still, with each of those examples, and with spirit connection as well, even the most educated and experienced teacher can only take you so far before you must take over the wheel and drive yourself past the threshold from novice to expert. You could watch an enlightened Reiki master alter the tension in a room or study miracle healings by a TV preacher—or mimic every move I make during a spirit reading—and ultimately, that observation and even our detailed instructions wouldn't have nearly the influence you might think.

That leads us to one elephant in the room of modern spiritual life: the online guru. Before the digital age, teachers were considered qualified if they'd had years of study toward a degree or decades offering instruction, whereas now a million views of a video or someone's trending catchphrase, hashtag, or status is enough for a person to become an influencer in every sense of the word. All of us with smartphones or computer access need to recognize that new global reality, whether we follow any particular person closely or not, as one of the sources of influence on our beliefs.

One prominent example, the pop spirituality hot topic of the law of attraction, is similar to the phenomenon of inner beliefs becoming real in an outer way. On its face, there is nothing wrong—and in fact much potentially good—in understanding the law of attraction and adopting it into our own beliefs. Where it veers into something quite different from the study of our spiritual power, however, is at the point on the path where the whole purpose of believing becomes "manifesting," as so many social influencers call the process of getting stuff we want by believing in it enough. This use of the concept lacks nuance, as our ability to know our own minds and beliefs has a more subtle, more inestimable role.

The importance of understanding what you believe helps you recognize where you are in relation to the communion with universal spiritual knowledge you're actually always seeking. If you've ever "manifested" a new car or a new partner only to find soon afterward that you still feel quietly dissatisfied, you know what I mean. While it's easy to get caught up in the enthusiasm and clever wordsmithing of many online teachers, it is also all too easy to forget their motivations may not line up well with your particular soul journey. The only route to knowing whether any teacher, guru, or influencer's inspiring content has value on your path is to know yourself as a unique body-mind-spirit apparatus.

Take an Inventory of Your Beliefs

With a more distinct and powerful belief set, you'll gain a more distinct and powerful spirit connection. What's more, the quality (or energetic nature) of your beliefs, for better or worse, will set the invisible boundaries within which you receive spiritual information. So taking an inventory of your beliefs is a valuable place to begin intentionally noticing and shaping your ever stronger foundation for the clearest and most helpful spirit messages to reach you and benefit your life.

Now's the time to crack open that beautiful journal your sister-in-law gave you for your birthday, with its abundant, wide-open pages that have been calling to you with a disquietingly mysterious assignment while you keep stashing it in your regifting pile. Too specific? Just me with that journal? OK, then, using any notebook, diary, or pad of paper you like, tab off a generous section of blank pages for your belief inventory; you'll return to this section with additions, revisions, and inspirations as you give your beliefs new and different attention, making the inventory increasingly unique to you over time.

Belief Inventory Step One: What I Believe and Why

On your designated paper, answer the following questions truthfully, given how you know yourself and what you genuinely think of each subject at present. Leave a few blank pages after your answer to each question so that you can note and elaborate on any changes to your answers over time:

- Where did I come from (i.e., what is the original source of my current life/existence)?
- What is the purpose of my interaction, conflict, and communion with other people?
- And with nature?
- What do I believe about life beyond the physical body's existence? Is there heaven, hell, total nothingness, or reincarnation?
- Are humans evolving for a purpose?
- What about the planet?
- Are humans and other parts of nature on separate evolutionary paths? If so, why?
- Where did each of these beliefs I hold come from?

Belief Inventory Step Two: I Believe and I Know

Over time let your belief inventory evolve through daily experience, the things you read and listen to, and especially your encounters with spirit as you progress through this book. Use the knowledge about yourself that you develop throughout this book's practices to cull your most essential beliefs from the inventory for daily use. Be willing to amend or release any beliefs that prove more burdensome than they're worth. Use the plentiful journal pages you've left open for each question to ponder, reevaluate, and affirm beliefs that level up with your new direct experiences of evidence. As soon as you're able to truthfully change a statement about spirit from "I believe that" to "I know that," you'll see some amazing positive effects in your ability to communicate in that realm.

A Word on Alignment

The conflict you go through over any given situation—wondering what to do, think, or deduce about yourself, another person, or life in general in reaction to it—is a matter of alignment between your soul's higher knowing and your earthly self's thoughts and physical actions. In our minds, we may feel utterly convinced a particular life choice is the right one but still end up with miserable tangible results. This very human fallibility appears when our belief inventory is still muddled with influences that contradict what our higher self naturally knows on the spiritual level. It's the reason my approach begins with tools for recognizing the daily interactions of your body, mind, and spirit.

Often instead of taking the time to do the work of a belief inventory or cultivate our cleanest physical state, we take shortcuts like denying or numbing ourselves to pain or seeking distraction. Sometimes we do this through vices that become addictions or even excessive goodness, like cultivating hyper-independence (never needing or asking for help) or a savior complex, which compels stepping in front of a train for every wounded bird—and telling ourselves and others half-truths. That last extremely common trap of misalignment shows up in the partial honesty of getting into a committed relationship with a safe partner we know doesn't truly ignite our soul or taking a new job for an impressive title and salary when our spiritual compass doesn't line up with the company's work. We may even be quietly trying to tell ourselves that our children will appreciate our long hours of work away from them for the material gifts we can offer them as a result.

But there's a Yiddish saying that goes, "A half-truth is a whole lie." And spirit knows the whole truth. As the lightest and therefore most sensitive gauge of the underlying quality of absolutely everything that takes place in our lives, it responds quickly and sparks the changes in our bodies and minds that demonstrate quite obviously when something is out of whack or when wellness is flowing abundantly. We therefore turn our attention next to understanding, feeding, and communicating through that most mysterious, subtle, yet powerful component of the body-mind-spirit apparatus—the ever-present tool of spirit. Let's uncover how each of us was born to engage its gifts in our living of every day.

3

Now, Your Spirit:
Let Reverence Lead the Way

Like distinct musical instruments coming together in a jazz trio—
each impressive on its own and in unity just plain magnificent—
the body, mind, and spirit coalesce when this third element of your
being, your spirit, takes the stage. While it's the star of this book, just
as a trumpet's notes carry through a room and out beyond the walls
when it joins the rhythmic structure from the drums and the tones of
the piano, our natural divine spirit in all its glow and pizzazz is also an
ensemble player.

If you've already been seeking some greater truth about life and
your part in it for a while, you've likely run across pronouncements like
"Everything in the universe is interconnected" and "Separation is merely an
illusion" from philosophers, religious and new-age teachers, and scientists—
all with their own form of evidence to back up their pronouncement. I'll
refer to some of the wonderful truths you and I can learn from that variety
of perspectives at times, but most of all, I'm going to ask you to jump
into that great wide-open, interconnected universe with your full human
apparatus of body, mind, and spirit engaged in discovery. Finding your own

evidence, directly and viscerally, for what those various experts are talking about is the reason you're here. You've had an instinct that spirit is the key to answers about yourself, whether in the form of messages from a loved one who's died or through a relationship with another form of spirit guide. Maybe you have no idea why you're drawn to connecting with spirit, like I didn't when I was a confused, silently tormented young wife and mother longing for divine guidance. Now after years of working with people from all walks of life and in all stages, I can give you a hint: the desire to connect with spirit is about no less than becoming your own best expert and feeling your link to everything else in the universe, firsthand, for yourself.

Whether we're focusing inward to tune in to who we are individually as a spiritual being or expanding our awareness outward to pick up the presence and messages of spirit in other forms, the essential energetic stuff we need to learn to pick up is the same. It's in us, in other beings, and throughout the natural universe. So while "spirit" is hard to define without leaning on analogies, metaphors, or recycled religious tropes (I'll admit I made the mistake of trying to do that in response to an online skeptic, just once), the inherent divine spirit in everything is always accessible to feel and engage with for ourselves. And isn't having a direct, personal connection really more valuable than being able to define it precisely for someone else anyway?

Please understand: I deeply value authentic skepticism and the path of questioning it spurs us to follow. I couldn't have developed my own ability to use and teach the gift of spirit communication without having felt my own healthy dose of skepticism along the way. But combatting any and every spiritual topic as manufactured nonsense isn't the same as healthy skepticism; I just call it missing out. The spirit component of your human apparatus is unique among the others in that it isn't something we can draw an accurate diagram of like a textbook can depict the parts of the body or the brain. Spirit is energy, which is invisible until it interacts and collaborates with matter and we can see its effects. And all creatures—including you here with this book, your family dog in the den, a murmuration of starlings in the sky, and a mother whale under the sea—are made up of just the right mix of matter and original divine source energy to be able to connect with it in others.

After decades of exploring my own and others' paths to discovering and interacting with spirit, I can, at the very least, point you in the right direction to see, feel, blend, and communicate with it yourself. I can even promise that you'll know divine spirit when you encounter it (and my kids can tell you that I'm cautious about making promises). Here's why I'm sure I can make that one: over and over, in many hundreds of sessions and thousands of everyday encounters, I've witnessed the spirit in a person light up with recognition when it comes in contact with the presence of spirit in anything else. I will teach you the best I can with words what that connection of spirits is like, but jumping in and swimming around in the essence of it yourself, without need for words, will be oh so much better.

Remember from the introduction that "spirit energy" is my broad term for the nonphysical aspect or silently communicative voice of life flowing through any object or being, including you. And just as it's linked linguistically through Latin to the word spirare, meaning "to breathe," spirit energy is a necessity of life. The longer I've served as a medium to convey the detailed messages of spirit, the more I understand an even starker truth: life is both the purpose and the expression of spirit.

You'll notice I distinguish divine spirit from spirit because we've come to use the word "spirit" for a lot of meanings—positive and negative, creative and destructive, life-affirming as well as blocked and twisted. We might say, "His spirits are really low after the breakup," or "She sent a mean-spirited letter," or one of the concerns I've heard more than a few times, "How do you guard against evil spirits?" But what I'm most concerned with is the original divine spirit, the universal flow of life force that is as powerful in your essential nature today as it was in the Big Bang from which you and I, and all of life as we know it, evolved. Some people call divine spirit God force; some call it prana or source energy or Christ consciousness or Brahman. Regardless of which story of the divine is most compelling to us, we're all deep down talking about the same thing: the goodness and light energy that propelled us here through our birth and remains (forever, as far as I can tell from hundreds of spirit readings) beyond our death.

As you proceed in the adventure of building direct relationships and communication with spirit throughout this book, keep in mind it's this divine life-force version of spirit I am talking about, in any of the bazillion forms it can take. Your soul is one of those forms, and it is always, without exception, a purely boosting and creative force for growth, evolution, and expansion. It's capable of promoting those things for you as well as for every other life form, as it's the part of you inextricably linked to everyone else. It can be hard at times for us to mentally acknowledge that divine spirit in others' lives. On their surface, the events, people, or natural phenomena that challenge our peace, stretch our endurance and patience, or trample our dearly held beliefs may seem anything but divine—or at least that is, until you stop to really ponder how essential such instigators are to change and progress. In essence, spirit is calling to you even more powerfully from within those big challenges, as a purely positive force in disguise, asking you to grow and showing you the way. Many of us come to newfound spiritual knowledge when we face major conflict or even what feels like rock bottom in our lives. Divine spirit is there too.

The Billboard You Can't Miss
on the Path to Divine Spirit

The greatest news I hope you'll discover through the tools and practices here is that our best trick for accessing divine spirit is not a trick at all; it's as much a part of our nature as breathing in and out. No matter what you may have heard from the movies, from the people who raised you, or from the Pope, there is no dogma you have to accept or ritual you need to perform to be able to commune directly and personally with the divine. This applies every day of your life, wherever you are and whatever you're doing.

In centuries past I would have been burned at the stake for making that claim, and in our current one, there are plenty of people who would still believe I should be. Although I'm not here to refute or fight them, I do take the knowledge that they're out there as reminder of my responsibility to make my statements with plenty of firsthand knowledge and backup evidence from others' experience of its truth. I also know, as our exploration of beliefs in Chapter 2 pointed out, that you yourself may have had past experiences that conditioned you to seriously doubt your direct access to divine spirit or its existence at all. So I'll suggest again here that you set aside those conditioning experiences for a brief while and let yourself ease back into a natural, childlike state of simply wondering what the truth might be. Remember to allow your belief inventory from the previous chapter to remain a breathing, evolving thing.

That wonder and curiosity—the buzzy, excited-about-the-possibilities kind that a second grader who's fascinated by outer space takes on a field trip to the planetarium—are the first hint you're on the fast route to connecting with spirit. The very best thing for you to learn here to cultivate, even if you don't feel it right now or in many other moments, is the sense of reverence that naturally follows opening yourself up to the possibility of spirit. Trust that we can get you to a reverence that will plunge you right into the stream of divine spirit more easily than you might think.

What do I mean by reverence? A feeling of profound admiration and desire to honor a higher power, an idea, a person, a marvel of nature, a work of art, even a dish of pasta. It can come over us at any time and in any place if we let it. Life naturally presents us with awe-inspiring, wondrous moments, and simply relishing them with reverence immediately orients us to the viewpoint our divine spirit perpetually holds. "Simply" delighting in any given moment does not necessarily come easily, of course. Whether you're devoutly spiritual or you've never had an access point to spirituality that made sense to you, there are subjects in your life about which your essential divine nature steadily nudges you toward reverence, while you firmly (and likely unknowingly) resist it. Unfortunately, negative thoughts, societal standards, and physical discomfort (those mind and body challenges we addressed in the first two chapters) make noisy companions, even when something glorious is around us and calling for our attention. Divine spirit most often speaks with a quiet voice, and most of us humans tend to listen to louder voices first. Whether the noise comes from the fears our parents have passed down, our culture's rules, our stomach's growls, or our children's needs, the competition for attention is stiff.

But here's some great news, an extra-fantastic bonus quality I've noticed about divine spirit: as long as I haven't let my mind or body become too clouded by negativity, I'm able to call divine perspective back into collaboration with my body and mind even when I'm feeling down or disconnected from it in a particular moment. The same way sense memory allows us to recall a moment of shame or hurt long after the injury to our pride occurred, even a minuscule glimpse of a sensation from a time I've synced in with the divine in the past is enough to call it right back into my physical experience at any given time.

While you experiment with the different ways reverence shows up uniquely in your body and mind, know that you already are communicating with divine spirit. As you progress through the rest of this book and its exercises, you'll learn to stretch and refine that ability into a power you don't have to just wonder about anymore—you'll know it, in clear and distinct detail.

So first things first: the stories and experiments in this chapter for cultivating reverence are to help you notice divine spirit flowing through both everyday and unexpected moments, appreciating them for the way they make you feel and the ways they inspire you to act. Especially if you're among the many people who look at the world today and have trouble coming up with much of anything you revere anymore, take this as a welcome opportunity to relieve that frustrating condition from the inside out. By the time you've dedicated yourself to some practical habits for welcoming more reverence into your daily experience, you'll have become aware of some very real and marvelous things about yourself and the world around you—the truth of which will inspire and empower you to become an ever more engaged participant in creating those wonders worthy of delight.

Getting Practical: Recognize and Amplify Reverence

SENSATIONS. Think about how you felt in school when that gorgeous classmate with the sparkling personality sat near you at lunchtime. It was pretty hard to eat while your heart pounded and your stomach fluttered, right? But it wasn't exactly a bad feeling either, was it? Depending on how young you were when you first felt an unmistakable sensation like one of those in your body, you might have been confused or even thought you were sick. These are common examples of the everyday way our bodies serve as tools for translating energy without our stopping to notice what a truly beneficial collaboration exists within our body-mind-spirit apparatus. A brief stomach flutter, ring in the ears, or tingle on the scalp can be a sensory sign alerting you to a moment of significant meaning to consider more closely.

Some years back a close friend of mine kept recommending a book about what a gift fear is to anyone who'd listen. From what I gathered, one message of this widely popular (we're talking Oprah's list) book was how to discern the nuanced bodily sensations that arise when there's something or someone threatening in your vicinity. I saw the value of learning to use our natural instincts to be safe from danger, but I also remember feeling a little sad that the angle gaining such popularity was so negative. What if we all paid that much attention to the nuanced messages our bodies give when something divine is in our vicinity? It's the same mechanism, turned toward the sunshine instead of the gloom. We have that prerogative of choosing how to angle ourselves, and you get a new chance to reorient your tools of perception in every moment.

The time you devote to developing your bodily awareness through posture, breathing, vigorous exercise, and the practice of slow, precise movements, like we covered previously, boosts your ability to pick up the subtlest changes of spirit energy in a given experience. That's why I begin all of my workshops with the body as our focus, to ensure you are at your most receptive place to pick up the sensations that signal the wisdom and guidance available to you, whether through the passive encounters I describe in Part II or the more active engagement with spirit in Part III.

For either situation, the higher the perspective you've nurtured into your spiritual environment through reverence, the more favorable and supportive the guidance you can access.

TRY THIS: Right where you are, take three deep breaths with each exhale lasting two counts longer than the inhale (meaning for example, breathe in for three counts and then breathe out for five), and then repeat this exercise two more times. As you get to the end of the third set of those full breaths, begin to focus on a memory of something you witnessed and thought was glorious, maybe watching an incredible performance or athletic competition, listening to a hope-filled speech by someone you admired, singing a song in a large group where everyone knew the words by heart, or seeing a new baby (human, giraffe, duckling, whatever) being born. The more intensely engaged you were with what you saw, the better. (Your rapt attention, actual physical participation, or close relationship to the object of your attention could hint at that intensity.) Let yourself fully dive back into that memory now, until you can feel the sensation of energy begin to balloon up in your chest as a feeling of warmth, a fluttering heartbeat, or a quickened breath, maybe even as the slightest burn of joyful tears welling up in the corners of your eyes. The deeper my dive with spirit has gone over the years, the more frequently I've noticed subtler, stranger sensations. Tingling on different specific spots of my scalp, rhythmic twitches in a toe or knee, a buzzing vibration in a single muscle area, and a swooping sort of dizziness are all sensations I've learned to associate with receiving specific divine content. If you're also particularly sensitive to energy, those sensations might be very familiar to you too.

I recommend you let yourself go to the furthest edges of positive emotion in this memory experiment, because at first, immersing in such intense divine energy (what our most marvelous experiences amount to, after all) can bring bodily sensations you might easily confuse with feelings of anxiety, nervousness, overwhelm, or even fear. Increased heart rate, for example, can happen in both scary and wonderful situations. The more you tune in to your body's sensations in a variety of circumstances, the better you'll get at discerning the difference between positive and negative spirit energy. The sensations of a positive experience often feel like a lift upward inside, as opposed to oppressive energy that pulls or presses down on you. Consider the difference of feeling you'd get if all of your internal organs were rising in excited anticipation as you reached the top of a roller coaster versus the sinking dread in the pit of your stomach you'd get if you had to take a test you didn't study for.

While you're experimenting with positive inputs, try to simply notice the moment you hook into a sensation you recognize as uplifting energy. When that happens, ever so subtly shift your focus to amplifying the sensation. You can intentionally grow that boosting, billowing feeling using the incredible power of your mind's eye until you're not paying attention to the specific details of the memory anymore but to the feeling of divine energy moving through you in response to the divine energy in those details that inspired your reverence. How marvelous is that? The energetic sensations of simply recalling a memory can effectively match the sensations your body felt when you experienced the original moment itself! I don't know about you, but the more I experiment with the consistency of that mechanism, the more I have to wonder at the miraculous way detailed yet formless spiritual content apparently travels outside the constraints of space and time.

In that practice, you have a hint at the marvel and delight you'll feel when you realize you're receiving detailed messages from a source who is in purely spiritual form!

EMOTIONAL COMPLEXITY. Interconnected with those physical sensations we get in response to divine encounters is a whole range of emotional signals. Our sensations of "being moved" energetically by something can also show up as an intensely emotional experience telling us we're in the midst of divine spirit. In those moments, we can sense our own inner spirit is responding with both recognition and reverence to the details of the divine's real and powerful appearance in another form. But just as the divine may be closely associated with great joy, it can be reflected just as well in tenderness or powerful loyalty. The common thing underneath these varied and wildly different positive emotions is deep and unconditional love.

So let's talk about that sort of love. It's not all roses.

When I recently traveled to stay with some friends I consider my family in Portland, Oregon, we dove one lazy afternoon into a conversation about how the divine shows up in our lives. This was right at a time when we each happened to be watching our own youngest child embark on a huge life-phase transition, and as we discussed the way our children have unwittingly brought us face to face with divine spirit, Cadence, my graceful-souled best friend of thirty years, pointed out something I hadn't ever put together in such elegant words: "Sure, we recognize divine spirit by the pure reverent love we feel. But add a tinge of sad emotion in it too. Delight and poignancy—the corporal, temporal nature of the moment. Holding the eternal and the impermanent at the same time creates a little bit of tension where you know you're in the liminal space of something divine."

You see why I stick around this girl?

The clarity Cadence's observation offers is that we can discern more complex qualities and details about our lives from divine spirit than simply good versus bad, happy versus sad. The more you become proficient with your emotional complexity, the further your spiritual vocabulary will take you in a whole range of subjects that matter to you.

AESTHETIC EXPERIENCE. Physical form is the integral aspect of our life that distinguishes it from any ethereal existence we might have before birth or after death, and in physicality, the array of aesthetic details we encounter provides rich ground for our reverence to germinate and grow. We may first think of aesthetics as pleasing visual details, but well beyond just seeing stirring colors, intriguing patterns, or remarkable contrasts in scale with our eyes, the more subtle senses of our layered body-mind-spirit apparatus give meaning to aesthetics too. Texture, tone, and ambience are examples of aesthetic qualities that are harder to isolate to a single sensory mechanism of awareness. And certainly someone without eyesight or hearing relishes countless aesthetic experiences even without one physical sense. Our natural-born tendency to translate a given mix of aesthetic details into a provocative emotional or transcendent moment hints at the divine spirit within us that is always ready to be awakened. That the aesthetic particulars that stir one person's spirit are not necessarily the same for the next is a sign of the great diversity of our universe, and that diversity itself is a wondrous aesthetic quality I love to contemplate for a fast track to reverence.

My friend Cadence's husband, Rob, shared with us during that recent afternoon in Portland that he has attached a combination of peace and awe, close relatives of reverence, to powerful aesthetic experience since reading *Way of the Peaceful Warrior*, in which Dan Millman describes relishing a simple meal in a café as the most delicious food he's ever tasted. Rob's point sent my mind immediately to my father—an architect and a passionate home chef whom the rest of the family and many friends tried to emulate every time we cooked. He'd sit back and marvel at an exceptional dish, sometimes after just a bite or two, and whether he'd prepared it himself or one of us had cooked, he'd declare, "That was the best thing I ever ate!" He meant it every time. I learned early on from my dad's honest delight at culinary feats (and at so many other creative works too) that loving attention and intention toward a piece of art, music, food, or writing can infuse it with an ineffable aesthetic power we can instantly recognize. Usually, words scarcely describe the effect in a way that does it justice. That almost unutterable yet still powerfully meaningful stuff of an aesthetic experience is what I refer to as the "spiritual content" of life.

Artists and architects demonstrate how passionately the human spirit responds to and embraces details of form, line, and texture, each manipulating those elements uniquely through their meticulous attention to craft that tends to set a great final product apart from less compelling work. The instinct to create something new for ourselves and others to enjoy for its aesthetics is pervasive. And we're not even the only members of the animal kingdom to craft objects of beauty that don't have any obvious purpose other than to be beautiful; look at the underwater crop circles of a pufferfish or intricately ornamented love nests of a bowerbird.[5] Maybe their potential mates experience that je ne sais quoi as they gravitate toward a specific structure the way we might find ourselves captivated by one painting more powerfully than another on a gallery wall. Or the way some of us thrill at the perfection of an extremely challenging crossword puzzle or football play sooner than at any fine art. The more you make it a point to notice even small aesthetic details that strike you as wordlessly powerful, the more you can be sure you're connecting to the universal divine spirit as it dwells right under your nose.

---

5 Jasmin Fox-Skelly, "The Animals with an Eye for Art," *BBC Future*, BBC May 30, 2022, https://www.bbc.com/future/article/20220527-the-animals-with-an-artistic-eye.

PREFERENCES. Along with your physical and emotional feelings, the interests, tendencies, and particular passions you have are great indicators of and receptacles for your reverence. You might not consider your strength in math class or devotion to rehabbing old cars to be divine pursuits, but spirit certainly does when your reverence for them is true and powerful. In those places and activities where you feel the most wrapped up and enthralled with what you're doing, you're in a state of being where spirit is most easily able to reach you with its quiet voice. You're paying attention to minute details. You feel care and interest in doing exceptional work or in furthering the hard work of generations before you. It's an awesome flow to be part of in any subject.

On my own journey of spiritual discovery, I cannot imagine having reached the levels of awareness of the divine I've encountered without my intimate relationship with music. I grew up in a family of musicians, both instrumental and vocal, so for all I knew from birth, learning, making, and living music were part of human nature. We sang in a round on car trips; sat at my dad's feet while he tried out the new banjo, accordion, or recorder he'd brought home; listened to my parents' choir friends who packed our living room to rehearse; and played our piano recital pieces for my aunts, uncles, and grandmothers, who all played instruments themselves. By the time I was an adult and had practiced pieces of music for hours too—both in solitude at the piano or with a clarinet or flute and as part of musical groups of souls pouring themselves into creating something bigger and more complex through collaboration—I knew I felt closest to divine perfection within the scale of notes that held endless potential.

For someone without any of that background in music, maybe it's hard to understand the reverence I feel when I turn on a recording of a classical cantata and try to match its alto section with my own voice as my dad always did with the basses. It's actually wonderful news that we don't all have the same preferences and proficiencies, isn't it? By wholeheartedly diving into your preferences regardless of others' opinions and discovering what in you resonates with those interests, you contribute to a heightened universal energy that ultimately uplifts all of us.

Elaine's Story: The Power of Nature

My longtime client Elaine hadn't thought of the love and connection she felt with animals as a form of reverence until I recently told her it might be one of the purest expressions of it I'd ever seen. But as she started recounting different important relationships she'd had with animals throughout her life, from beloved pets and rescued strays to the raccoons and birds that cross her yard every day, she began to hear herself rhapsodize. That time a lost dog was the reason she first knew her purpose for being alive. The way a cat she'd adored in a strange peer-to-peer way showed up in multiple spirit readings and synchronicities, helping Elaine release all skepticism about the truth of a higher power, which her analytical mind had always gripped to before. While she and I talked about these bonds as sacred, her eyes started to widen at the thought that animals had always been her single best conduit to the divine.

"It's like catching the end of a thread that traces back through your whole life and makes you realize it's always been there," Elaine said about the disarming recognition she's always felt with animals. "It was almost a primordial experience to be around them when I was a kid. I got a feeling of comfort that was different from anywhere else. And making that direct connection to nature brought other, difficult parts of my life into perspective every time." As she continued to speak on the topic, Elaine realized that each era of significant personal growth in her life had an animal at the center of the story.

The specificity of Elaine's soul-level connection with certain animals is a beautiful example of the way a strong personal preference, no matter how common or peculiar, reveals the divine spirit coursing through us in specific form.

A Natural Starting Place

You may not be at a stage in your life when you feel very clear about your specific passions and preferences. We will look at the many spiritual stages we go through, and I hope it reassures you that even a state of "the blahs" where you can't feel much reverence is more than OK. However, for the sake of priming your body-mind-spirit apparatus for all there is to uncover later, let's consider the story I shared about Elaine from a more universal viewpoint. As human beings, even those of us who live mostly surrounded by concrete, metal, and plastic, we are all part of the earth's varied and dynamic ecosystems, and so nature itself is the most fundamental and accessible place to uncover your sense of yourself as spirit.

Many of us have felt something like bliss when we've spent time in nature, and lots of academic research backs the scientific benefits. Nature journalist Richard Louv, author of ten books and a leader in the international movement to connect children and families with nature, writes, "An increasing number of physicians—particularly pediatricians and psychologists—are no longer satisfied that pharmaceuticals and traditional counseling alone can reverse the social isolation, depression, and substance abuse experienced especially by young people. Some now write 'nature prescriptions' to encourage families to spend more time outdoors."[6]

Can you imagine your doctor jotting those orders on her prescription pad and sending you on your way? The image is enough to light me up with reverence for research, that's for sure. Thankfully, though, not everyone needs a doctor to tell them this stuff. Even (and I'd say especially) in places where industry and technology are obscuring the natural ecosystem's intimate role in our lives, we feel soul-level instincts reminding us of our interconnection with the natural environment. Indigenous cultures worldwide have always incorporated a sense of kinship with nature into their ways of life, celebrating and protecting natural resources for generations to follow. As a child, I remember feeling that natural kinship as a really uncomfortable, antsy urge to get outside if I was cooped up too long in a windowless or overly air-conditioned room. My whole being seemed to know where it wanted to be.

A simple 2016 study from St. Catherine University seemed to back the spiritual call of nature as well.[7] Researchers asked twenty-six adults to spend fifteen minutes per day over ten days immersing themselves in nature and reflecting on its effects on the spirit through photography and journaling. Its authors explained, "Six main spiritual themes emerged from thematic analysis: connection, vibrancy, awe/presence, joy, gratitude, and compassion. Of these six themes, the findings revealed that immersion in nature impacts the human spirit most significantly by providing a sense of connection, vibrancy, and awe." Even further, the authors wrote, "regardless of the type of nature activity, the location, or the time of day, immersion in

6 Richard Louv, "Our Species Loneliness." North Cascades Institute (blog), November 13, 2019, https://blog.ncascades.org/naturalist-notes/our-species-loneliness/.
7 Schauer, Becky, Kishori Koch, Laura Lemieux, and Kendra Willey, "How Immersion in Nature Impacts the Human Spirit: A Phenomenological Study." Retrieved from Sophia, the St. Catherine University repository website, May 2016, https://sophia.stkate.edu/ma_hhs/8.

nature offered a sense of connection for every participant, which in turn promoted spiritual well-being."

You may not be sure at your present stage how strongly you feel about art or sports or global cuisine. It's possible that you didn't grow up with adults demonstrating awe, reverence, or wonder at much of anything. Even if every example in this chapter of the spirit's role has left you a little baffled, we do all have at least a little experience with nature. If it's all you try out of this entire book, try watching the sky for fifteen minutes a day over ten days in a row and see what awakens in you.

Part 2

Your Everyday Encounters with Spirit

4

Signs: Recognize Spirit's
Many Different Forms

One weekday afternoon, a client of mine sat in a power suit and expensive heels at a café with her cell phone to her ear and a double espresso on the table in front of her. This woman is remarkably refined and smooth on the outside, with every hair in place and a businesslike voice even in casual conversation. As she spoke to a colleague on the phone, she blended in well with the upper-class clientele streaming by without looking at her. Suddenly, a man with short gray hair and a tattered shawl-collar sweater approached and held out his hand to her without a word. Hardly thinking about the interaction as she responded, she opened her own hand to him and he placed a tiny object in it before walking away. As she wrapped up her call, she looked down to see a small decorative key in her hand. It had the word "HOPE" etched into its long side. At this, the woman let out a small gasp and silently started to cry.

How did the stranger, who'd already disappeared down the sidewalk, know my client was at the end of her rope that day, in repressed turmoil over her husband's drug addiction and the possible end of her marriage? And what were the chances the stranger had this key at the ready as he walked by her, when she'd had a small tattoo since college with the word "HOPE" etched along her lowest rib, now hidden under her suit?

Or what about the many people who've told me they knew someone close to them had died because the person had appeared in a dream full of light and reassurance in the hours before the news arrived? And the countless silent moments of astonished recognition other clients have had while traveling through their days—one glimpsing a mascot animal on a billboard the same day a college letter announced admission; another noticing the exact car model a distant ex used to drive with a dashboard hula girl just like his, only to see a text message pop up from him an hour later; another pressing "shuffle" on a music app and immediately hearing her brother's favorite song on the anniversary of his death?

The curiosity about spirit that brought you to this book is enough to tell me you've also likely had your share of encounters that have taken you by surprise and didn't quite make sense to you. Those odd, beautiful, startling moments you can't explain without a quiet voice inside wondering whether it was a spirit appearance are, indeed, the day-to-day signs that we're part of a much vaster web of connection than many of us have been taught to acknowledge. And again, the confidence I have in claiming this truth with conviction comes from my direct personal experience with that web over many years. You too have the natural tools to know the intricate and supportive strength of the web for yourself firsthand.

Your Five Senses, In Spirit Form

In the very first sentence of Chapter 1, I asked if you remember learning your five senses in kindergarten. Of all the essential knowledge we absorbed in our formative childhood years, I wish the lessons on our senses would carry on a lot further. Knowing how quietly powerful we become when we tune more subtly into the nuances of our senses, I have to wonder why we don't ask children what they're able to notice just beyond what they hear, taste, see, smell, and feel. In some cultures—mainly populations still connected to their indigenous roots that are, in turn, well rooted to the specific natural ecosystem in which they've long dwelled—children are raised to know and use those abilities. Serving many purposes from physical survival to higher spiritual wisdom, our more nuanced senses are as important and inherent as the material ones.

Among the psychic mediums I felt both reluctant and compelled to join and study years ago when my own senses seemed to be going haywire, I learned the extrasensory tools for picking up spirit all have names corresponding with physical senses. Each name begins with the prefix "clair-," meaning "clear" in French, and these less understood senses are where our greatest—and quietest—clarity is found. I like to think more specifically of "transparence," or the allowing of light to pass through so that details may easily be perceived. Considering we are all made up of millions of atoms that are 99 percent open space, I'm able to conceive of myself literally seeing, hearing, and feeling easily through and beyond objects. It is there in the clear, just-beyond place where these expansive versions of our physical senses take us that our day-to-day relationship with divine spirit resides. Here is how each distinct spiritual sense functions for your benefit, each word defined in parentheses with a conventional label in quotes followed by my own words for describing the firsthand experience:

1. Clairvoyance ("clear seeing" or perception beyond eyesight). As the most commonly used of these terms, clairvoyance is also probably the most misused. Thanks to the dramatic possibilities, pop culture has swept

the broad idea of extrasensory abilities into this one catch-all word, usually as an ability to see the future. The real capacity and purpose of clairvoyance may not be as catchy, but it is a visionary power we all have and can develop to serve our lives profoundly.

Clairvoyance is your ability to see with your mind's eye, whether your physical eyes are open or closed. The appearance of colors in the energetic space around an object or person, the flash of a person's face who isn't physically there, or the running of a story reel full of vivid elements that you haven't actually seen happen, any of these common occurrences are the appearance of spiritual information through clairvoyance. Sometimes the content does in fact happen in real experience later on, and sometimes it is a more metaphorical vision of events or relationships. The ability to see visions is the easy part, while the translation of what we've seen is more complicated and only improves with practice, trial, and error.

TRY THIS: When you first wake up in the morning, for at least three minutes put aside the urge to check your phone or hop up and start the day. Close your eyes and breathe with intention while you think of the backs of your eyelids as movie screens. To fine-tune this "seeing" even further, let your eyeballs drift up slightly so that it feels like you're focused on the space behind the spot between your eyebrows. Gently set free any thoughts that creep in about your to-do list or worries that crop up about yesterday's conflicts, and simply watch. As soon as a picture or flashing thought of an object or person appears, welcome it to show you a bit more. Never push, pull, or cajole spiritual information. It is subtle and slippery until we let ourselves dive fully into it without expectation. Jot a few notes in your journal each day of these first-thing-upon-waking visions. Over time, you can look back at the type of visions you tend to receive, whether they are predictive or more complex and metaphorical. As your habit to journal about them accumulates, you will enhance your eventual ability to discern which are the especially meaningful visions you receive (at other times of day as well).

2. Clairaudience ("clear hearing," or the perception of language and sound beyond the ears). Our hearing is a wonderful way for spirit energy to reach us in both blatant and subtle form, because sound is simply energetic vibration moving through a transmission medium. It is our reception and perception of that vibrational wave that make it a sound. You know the old tree-falling-in-the-woods question? Without anyone there to hear it, the energetic vibration of the fall is only a vibration. The listener is the key to that event becoming a sound. If you've noticed much more subtle "sounds" than anyone else is able to hear around you, you're experiencing the extrasensory ability of clairaudience. That version of hearing is an especially good indicator of what a highly sensitive instrument your body-mind-spirit apparatus is, and it can be confusing to discern its purpose at first.

As a child I tried to describe for my parents the voices of other people I could hear over my own thoughts at times. My parents may have been too busy to hear me or might have dismissed my revelations as typical childish imaginings, but eventually that extrasensory experience became more refined and entirely central to my ability to communicate spirit messages for my clients. If you've had a song pop into your head for no apparent reason, or a person's name or another seemingly random word sticks on repeat in that part of your brain that translates audible sounds, you may be receiving a sign from spirit with special meaning worth considering. The specific associations you have with whatever you heard are the best place to start determining meaning. The memories, emotions, or connections that come up become the trail of clues for what spirit is conveying to you.

3. Clairalience ("clear smelling," or scent beyond smelling through the nose). In the same way our brain's receptors for sound can pick up signs

from the quiet source of spirit, some people encounter distinct smells that don't seem to be coming from any physical thing. You may be in a closed room and notice a sudden waft of gardenias that transports you to playing in your grandmother's backyard as a child, while nothing in the room could be giving off that scent. I've had the smell of cigarettes tell me in a spirit reading that the person I'm connecting with was a heavy smoker, astounding the client (and me) because no one nearby was smoking. Often associated with a specific person or time in our lives, our scent memories quickly bring up the vibrant presence of a significant moment or connection.

Personally, I'd probably choose this form of spirit sign as the most awe-inspiring and delightful. (I mean, how do they do that?) Having grown up in a rationality-driven community of scientists, I've had to remind myself and accept that it is more than OK not to understand exactly how something occurs even when you know from observation that it does, in fact, happen all the time. By paying close attention to how you experience smell throughout your day, you can enhance your ability to notice spirit presence through clairalience as well. Take in the most subtle differences in scents: compare the scent of a lemon to that of a lime; inhale the scent of the pages emitted by a brand-new book and compare the smell to that of an old one; or smell your baby's hair and compare its scent to that of your older child's hair. Picking up slight nuances is the way you'll receive most spirit messages in any form!

4. Clairgustance ("clear tasting," or the knowledge of flavors beyond the tongue). Experiencing this extrasensory version of taste is very similar to a clairalience experience and equally astonishing when you realize the flavor you're aware of is not coming from anything you actually have in your mouth. I have not experienced spirit through clairgustance more than once or twice, and I don't hear others' anecdotes about it as often as I do the

other forms of receiving spirit signs. However, the possibility is quite real that you might encounter a moment when an inexplicable flavor leads you down that trail of clues that spirit uses to show us meaning.

5. Clairsentience and claircognizance ("clear feeling" and "clear knowing," or awareness just beyond emotion and thought). These two powerful "clair" senses that I've saved for last require the same level of inner confidence to experience them in a practical way. They're apt partners in form as well: clairsentience is the awareness of feelings and emotions through energetic, spiritual content, while claircognizance is the awareness of knowledge through spirit—details you'd have no rational, material way to know. "Empathy" and "instinct" are the street terms for these senses, and most people use them every day without giving a thought to the mechanism at work.

Essentially, it may not matter whether you knew not to take a left turn down a certain street because your body's keen sensory organs picked up danger before your brain registered the reason, or because your guardian angel grandfather was giving you the nudge in the form of a pointed vibrational message to turn away from that road. The important result is your trust in the subtle information shared and your choice to act on it, which tells us the value of this sensory ability. The longer I've worked with individual clients over the years on their spiritual journeys and seen countless complete strangers in spirit reading sessions, the more convinced I am that we all have specific spirit beings—ancestors, animals, angels, fairies, higher selves, you name them—assisting with this extrasensory knowing and feeling of truth-just-beyond-evidence. The details I'm able to convey from the presence of a certain spirit energy are too detailed for the listener to deny—we are not left to navigate our lives alone in our most important moments. The evidence is available to you too.

TRY THIS: Noticing signs from spirit out in the world throughout your day calls for a light touch, energetically speaking. You are already a natural receptacle for such signs without having to reach for them or force anything. To keep your energy light on the subject, try considering it play. I'll call my favorite game to share with clients who feel cut off from their ability to flow with spirit energy "Noah's Ark."

When I was little, the Bible story of the man tasked with loading every kind of animal on earth onto a boat in pairs fascinated me. I already had some sense of nature's immeasurable diversity and bounty, so how could Noah have had space for them all—and, more importantly, kept them from eating each other? The point is that the variety in the animal kingdom has continued to delight me, so for this game, I choose an animal in my mind when I set out in the morning. Whatever comes to me first as a fleeting thought is the animal I go with. It's an especially great choice when the animal isn't one I consider likely to cross my path where I live (whale, giraffe, and giant tortoise are examples). The rest of the game is up to spirit; I simply ask to see that animal somewhere on my travels and remain open to the form it takes. When you try this game for yourself, resist the urge to dart your eyes all over the place in search of your animal. Let it in the way you would allow an instinct to turn you right instead of left, to cause you to eat a peach instead of a plum, to nudge you to look up from your phone and take in the environment around you.

Your Spiritual Culture

While exploring your strengths from among that list of "clair" senses builds your awareness for the variety of forms that spirit signs take, discernment of their context is also vital to the process of interpretation. The contextual details of spirit connections for different people always absolutely delight me. They reinforce what a specific and individual matter our relationship with divine energy is, which to me is evidence that every one of us has the attention and interest of the divine, no matter what. I call the ecosystem of that specific relationship your "spiritual culture," as your personal context is part inherited and part all you. Ultimately, the color and texture of your life's artwork might come from the same paint and brushes that your neighbor's do, but the rich expression of that masterpiece is unique to you.

Your spiritual culture is that landscape on which the what and the why of the spirit signs you receive will become apparent. As such, you won't line up (resonate energetically) with the signs of a spirit presence unless they have life context for you to recognize and eventually understand them. I say "eventually" because often we encounter spirit in ways that confuse or even scare us in the moment because we haven't yet learned the expansive perspective toward life and ourselves that will allow us to understand beyond the confining rules of reality usually handed to us. Our family background and the focus of our education are significant early influences on our spiritual context for translating signs. And yet, evolution beyond those influences is always possible (and healthy and natural), empowering your highest self-realization over time.

Consider the example of American Sign Language as a parallel for how different people might learn to communicate with spirit. With little exposure to the lives of people with hearing loss, I grew up unaware that the evolution of this expressive form includes many variations, such as Black ASL, which developed out of the early segregation of deaf schools in the United States. Signs developed certain meaning in one learning context that would be misunderstood or ignored in another. Some signs have changed to reflect broader cultural shifts too, like the motion of answering a cell phone has replaced the old thumb-and-pinkie spread gesture that used to demonstrate a landline receiver. Place and time both shape sign language motions: a person who grew up with deaf parents in Cincinnati and learned the signs of their 1960s school uses different signs than a parent in San Francisco learning ASL today from YouTube tutorials. These many distinctions end up having a powerful effect on the individuals' physical language culture. Along with geographic, racial and ethnic, political, and gender differences between people that result from our evolving in different environments, still more minute differences show up between people from the same environments as well.

Individuality Reigns in Spirit

The unique inner wiring that made you you from birth is the other major player forming your spiritual culture to determine the type and content of spirit communication you receive. Your individuality is that set of factors I devote the most space and attention to throughout this book because it happens to matter most from divine perspective as well.

The idea of soul-level individuality is obvious to anyone who grew up with siblings in the same household with the same parents but experienced the whole thing quite differently from what their sisters and brothers took away from that shared childhood. No matter how many people we surround ourselves with for emotional and material support, our most essential, spirit-energy self stands independently and at a specific angle to interact with the rest of existence in our own way. The fully grounded and practical expression of your individuality will also be our focus when we dive into what the universe is calling for from you. At this stage, learning to recognize your unique variety of signs from spirit will lay a strong foundation for you to later see roles for yourself that you might not have considered to be a fit before; it will allow divine spirit to provide the affirmation and boost you need to take new risks; and it will reassure you that independence does not mean disconnection from companionship and love.

TRY THIS: The best way I know to start recognizing the characteristics of your individual spiritual context is to keep some record of the spirit signs you notice. You can use your journal and make this practice a habit of jotting down any encounter that fills you with awe, reverence, and wonder about what (or who) was behind what you experienced. Use your "clair" senses to describe what happened and any thoughts about what it meant to you. Over time, you'll be able to add more analysis of the patterns you see. Are your signs more

- Symbolic/metaphorical or on-the-nose literal?
- Full of modern or ancient references?
- Subtle or blatant in how they reach you?
- Traditional to your background or iconoclastic in content?
- Reflective of the past or visionary toward the future?

Add your own questions and comparisons to become the driver of your unique learning process. When you make it your habit to look this carefully into everything spirit is offering you through signs and the ways you're interpreting them, you'll probably begin to notice that the frequency and richness of the signs are growing along with your awareness.

Alicia's Story: The Power of Heritage

Some of my childhood friends reappeared in my life during the time my abilities as a medium became very active and public, letting me know it was actually possible to reshape lifelong connections after sharing something I'd thought was largely unacceptable to the community I'd come from. In fact a few friends, like Alicia, went beyond asking me to do a spirit reading for them and over time have revealed in our conversations the extent of their own gifts for spirit communication. Alicia's abilities and the distinct nature of the signs she receives are beautiful representations of a unique spiritual culture, and her openness about them is a model for all of us who know her to proudly reveal own our quirky distinctions.

Likely the most stirring, compelling spirit signs Alicia has received have been the synchronistic and repeated visitations of three specific animals at critical moments in her life: an eagle, a mountain lion, and a snake. They've shown up dramatically and even violently at times, making it impossible for her to ignore their presence, both with their own unmistakable natural power and through the cultural symbolism associated with them.

Still, it did take some time for Alicia to realize that the three animals' appearances might be interrelated and meaningful specifically to her—that is, until her father casually mentioned the Inca Trilogy to her, and her eyes opened to rich layers of meaning. He explained that to the Incas, the ancient people of Peru, elements of nature were the embodiment of divine beings. In their pantheistic belief system, the sacred order of the universe was embodied by the condor (representing the divine world of the gods), the puma (the ambassador of earthly living), and the serpent (the harbinger of the world of the dead). At the time Alicia began running into these three creatures in close succession on her own home property, her life happened to be intensifying in ways that brought to the surface her deepest longings to understand her own place in an eternal natural order.

A few things to know about Alicia: She grew up in a comfortable middle-class upbringing as the only child of a Caucasian mother and Mexican American father with Indigenous heritage. Her parents encouraged Alicia's individuality as well as, if not better than, most parents did in our highly driven, intellectual community. After succeeding in college and law school and then holding a lucrative position in a law firm, Alicia set some major life changes into motion when she and her husband purchased a hillside property where they began building a new home and small farm to share with their young daughter. While finishing their house and learning the ropes of tending successful crops, cultivating the ancient grains indigenous to the property, raising goats, chickens, turkeys, and other auxiliary animals (thanks to Alicia, I now know rabbits control food waste and fertilize vegetables better than anything!), Alicia transformed into both the fierce caretaker and the relentless entrepreneur her soul knew itself to be. With the transformation, she also began to experience a lot of destruction in her life, as many spiritual warriors do on their journeys—the crumbling of old relationship patterns, routines, and external, material world expectations. Later we'll talk more about relishing others for all of their (sometimes hidden) gifts. Still, though beautiful in its divinity and authenticity, the process can be excruciating. After her divorce and a string of both toxic and miraculous new connections made in the course of running her farm as a single mom, Alicia can attest to that.

Enter the puma (or, to this region, the mountain lion). It started appearing on Alicia's surveillance videos from the cameras trained on the various corners of her foothill property. Through the observations of her neighbors she confirmed the animal was stalking livestock close to homes, as its natural prey in the mountains was succumbing to the same environmental changes that were making it hard for Alicia and fellow farmers to grow crops. One night, Alicia woke up in the dark to ghastly shrieks. It only took her a moment to recognize they weren't coming from ghosts but goats. The small herd she'd been raising since stewarding their births with her own hands was under attack. Without a spouse to help or a gun to reach for (and knowing, anyway, that the puma was under special protection by state law), Alicia ran up her hill and with a pitchfork and the help of a neighbor valiantly defended the goats, chasing the predator away at her own acute risk. After, while still flooded with adrenaline, she nursed her goats that had been fatally wounded by the mountain lion until she was sure she'd lost them.

In the days afterward, operating from stunned grief, Alicia went about rebuilding and reinforcing the enclosure she had once carefully researched and designed to prevent exactly the disaster that had just occurred. She worked her land, tended her remaining, visibly traumatized goats, and relived the fearsome encounter with every phone call from concerned friends and neighbors. During that physical and emotional recovery, a lone golden eagle—a raptor relative of the condor—followed Alicia's movements around the farm. At first she barely noticed its circles in the sky above her, but as it approached more closely, perching on a fence post near her tomatoes or landing on the eaves of her house at an odd angle, she couldn't help but see it was keeping vigil, and seemingly over her. Certainly this bird of prey had natural business on her farm as well and Alicia was worried it might find a way to get at her rabbits, even though they lived in a sound enclosure. But no, instead the eagle kept to the free-range rodents, reptiles, and birds on the slope for its meals and spent its free time politely shadowing Alicia.

By now you've probably guessed: that same year, Alicia also noticed a rattlesnake begin to haunt her. It persistently hunted around her chicken coops, where, thanks to Alicia's studious husbandry, eggs in a rainbow of colors were abundant. The snake slithered out across her path while she climbed her hill to collect potatoes, and it darted out of corners of her garage as if trying to get noticed. As traumatizing as her collision with the mountain lion had been, this reptile's sneaky, incessant presence was another test altogether. At the time, Alicia was also embroiled in a passionate new relationship fraught with drama, distrust, and threats. She was struggling for air, and her life seemed to keep pulling her down deeper by the ankles. Each startling appearance by the rattlesnake sparked her rage, until one day when it came up from the ground too close to her animal enclosures and she managed to bisect it with a flat shovel.

What of this triumvirate holding court around Alicia, her property, and her animals during such a tumultuous, draining period of her life? They seemed to heighten the energy around her even more when it would seem things were crazy enough. But could that heightening be the key to their spiritual signs? Thanks to the cultural connection she felt instantly with the Incan way of being and seeing divine messages in nature, Alicia was able to draw new layers of meaning from the day-to-day adversaries she was facing—with a snake, puma, and raptor providing perfect embodiment of the realms of death, earthly life, and heavenly existence she was pondering for herself through her greatest life transition so far.

Recognition Is the (Essential) Beginning

Sometimes when I'm introducing a new workshop group to the idea that they too can communicate daily with a variety of spirits, I think about the fascinating studies showing how unreliable witness memory is in reconstructing a crime. While we're going about our daily, livin'-in-a-material-world business, we're unlikely to notice a very specific detail and register it in our memory if we don't also recognize its weighty significance in the moment. Only when passersby get plunked on the witness stand and grilled about an event some months or even years later do they become aware a certain detail was weighty; then they try to reconstruct what they saw into the context of whatever meaning they've inferred from being called as a witness. That backward approach leads to inauthentic witness testimony, and it's not great for connecting authentically with spirit either.

Returning to the ASL example, if you aren't deaf and don't run across deaf people often, you may think of sign language as a monolith of certain specific motions that may look too strange and confusing for you to even try interpreting them. In the same way, if you don't spend numerous hours in intentional spirit communication, as I do with my clients, you might not have considered the countless different spirit signs and spiritual cultures there are. Apart from identifying where you stand on religion or the spiritual modalities that have begun to take on their own lore, I'm willing to bet you've never thought about the truth of a unique spiritual culture and set of spiritual gifts all your own that are shaping your interaction with the universe at all times. Knowing you have a spiritual identity that's entirely between you and the divine is major. And you're going to like what happens when you become the number one expert on it.

Before we go any further, it will serve you well to pause and make a deal with yourself, and make it again daily. "Self," you can say, "let's set out on this adventure by first recognizing the divine significance of all we are going to encounter on this day. From this open-eyed, eager start, we're sure gonna catch some magical signs meant just for us." There—now you're ready to proceed knowing you have divine spirit in your corner. And you're also getting good at talking to yourself. (They say the most brilliant people do.)

5

Songs: Learn Spirit's Favorite Languages

Now that you know there are endless ways that you—with your unique natural senses and distinct spiritual culture—connect each day with spirit energy with its many forms and signs, let's talk about interpretation. After all, most of us aren't fully satisfied just to know spirit is present or that our loved ones' lives continue in new form beyond death. We ultimately want to know what their divine perspective has to say about us and our lives. Seem a little selfish to admit? I have worked with hundreds of people and their spirit messengers, and by now I know well that it's not only OK to follow that selfish instinct, it's called for. You can think of the desire as self-reflective. Human beings are naturally curious about what our experiences of the world say about us. We take everything as a mirror of sorts, because from our souls' deep knowing, we're always meant to improve the ways we're showing up as humans and, in turn, to improve the quality of those experiences coming back to us.

I'm certain this self-reflective instinct is strong in you. It shows up in the most frequent questions I hear from clients and friends about spirit:

Why do different kinds of messages show up from different spirit forms to different people? And how do we know a particular message is coming from divine energy and not some untrustworthy or even dangerous source? Both questions get right to the importance of interpretation. For good discernment in interpreting spirit signs, we need to become fluent in—or at least recognize a few phrases of—the languages that spirit speaks. As we've already discussed, the divine will meet you where you are with signs you can see, feel, or hear from your context. But to understand their meaning, you're asked to go a little further. To know the language of spirit, you have to be willing to step into a strange land, to feel like a foreigner until you recognize through meaning that you're actually home.

My Story: The Power of Passion

When I was a teenager I became enthralled by the idea of going to Italy as an exchange student after an older girl in my high school showed slides at an assembly from her experience. My family had abundant blessings but wasn't the kind of rich most of my high school community was. We weren't the kind of people who spent summers in Europe or flew to Aspen for ski trips. Flying on a plane at all was rare during my childhood. My vacations involved piling into a hand-me-down Chevy and riding across agricultural plains to see our relatives in Wisconsin, or winding up a California mountain to squeeze into a tiny cabin some church friends welcomed us to share with them. So when I was sixteen, the thought of flying across a continent and an ocean by myself to find out how I would do in a place where the people and culture were all strange to me would not let me go. I couldn't shake it, though I didn't quite know why.

For teenage me, one of Italy's biggest draws was its language. Sounding just a breath outside the bounds of Spanish (which was comfortable and familiar to me from years of classes and its constant presence around my California home), Italian was a beguiling mystery. A Romance language in more than name, I was sure. Its syllables, gestures, and curvy pronunciation held everything that was the opposite of my safe home, small city, and straitlaced school.

Through a series of fortunate events—ones I now call divine intervention—my application was accepted to the American Field Service exchange program. The local AFS chapter awarded me a full scholarship, and the program assigned me to stay with a family in Agliana, Italy, a small town in the Tuscany region. I would go the summer I was seventeen, stopping first in New York for an orientation where I'd be one of fifty American teens from all over the country staying in dorms on the SUNY Stony Brook campus and listening as eager young teachers tried to groom us into gracious foreign guests.

Only about an hour of the orientation was about speaking Italian. Besides teaching us the first sentence we should say to our host families on arrival, the main gist of that seminar was "Make good use of your phrase books and throw yourself into speaking Italian. Don't be afraid to mess up. The people you meet will appreciate it."

I did, and they did.

All of the positive stereotypes I'd picked up before about Italians' overwhelming hospitality, passionate communication, bold expression, and unmatched aesthetic sensibility turned out to be true. My Italian-English dictionary and phrase book were vital because no one in my host family spoke any English except for a son who wouldn't return home from his own exchange trip in the United States until a few weeks into my stay. By the time he arrived, the lifeline he could offer me to translate my native language wasn't as crucial as I'd thought it would be. I'd gotten quick with the dictionary at all times of day or night, and my understanding of Spanish served me very well to gather the intent and meaning behind even the most mysterious words. The beauty of a culture that speaks with the hands, eyes, shoulders, and varying pace is that a foreigner has more cues from which to derive understanding.

What the return of my host brother, Vieri, changed most significantly about my time in Italy was the access my new friends and family now had, through him, to know me even better. He could work around translating the valiant but labored Span-talian I'd been using, and I watched the community's delight at having an American girl in the neighborhood grow as I became a more complete picture to them. The teenagers in town called to me to join their circles; the tiny grandmother in our household, Nonna Giulia, always served me something extra at meals; and my host parents took me around to meet their friends in the community. A tall boy named Fabio learned from Vieri that I had a big crush on him, and one night soon after, Fabio pulled me aside, asked me about California, and told me he couldn't believe I'd never spoken Italian before that summer. I'd barely constructed a reply when he swept me into a long, strong, memorable kiss. The other friends hanging out nearby teased us relentlessly after that, of course, but even their ribbing encircled me with a distinctly Italian insistent affection.

Never before those months had I become known and beloved outside the context of my hometown identity, where I was the little sister, the scholarship kid, the good girl. Without the luxurious vowel sounds, passionate gestures, and earthy camaraderie that Italian culture demanded I try that summer, I don't know if my mind would have cooperated to set my spirit free too, to be seen—and to see myself—in a new, free state.

The night I had to say goodbye to my new circle of friends, a strange thing happened. After hugs and promises exchanged in Italian to write each other letters (no swapping Instagram accounts back then!), I saw that tall and gorgeous Fabio had stationed himself near the car door where my host father was waiting to take me and my new siblings home. Fabio hugged and kissed me on both cheeks with good wishes and *"Ciao! Arrivederci!"* like everyone else had, only he stopped and held on to my shoulders a second longer and looked right into my eyes.

"Ehi . . ." he said, and waited until I was looking straight back at him. *"Comanda, no?"*

With his imploring look, the sudden disappearance from my awareness of everything else around us, and the dramatic but strange words coming out of his mouth, the moment could have come from one of my favorite romance movies, except it made my heart pound even harder. It was, however, over in a flash as I got into the car. And like with many things people had said to me at the goodbye, I reflexively checked with Vieri to translate Fabio's words as we rode away. But while I watched my new friends and Fabio go back to roughhousing and dancing on the sidewalk like we had together every night that summer, I was sure inside I already knew the translation.

"Comanda . . . It's 'lead,'" Vieri told me. To clarify, he poked the air with his nose straight toward me. "You—lead."

New Languages Stir Our Souls Awake

That single word that a boy in Italy said to me decades ago stuck in my mind and has stayed in my soul, in large part because of the unfamiliar, passionate new languages I'd learned to embrace before I could fully understand them. Not only the Italian language itself, but a new body language, the emotional and aesthetic languages of the people hosting me. We know from neuroscience that learning a new spoken language gets our brains' synapses firing to create new neural pathways that make us more efficient thinkers. It essentially becomes an act of understanding and managing multiple approaches to communication at the same time. There is even a substantial body of scholarly research investigating whether and how becoming bilingual may be correlated with empathy. So it's no wonder to me that some of my most affecting encounters with spirit also have come through moments of stretching into and inhabiting a new language, spoken or otherwise. Broader and more portentous meaning can blossom out of that newly multifaceted awareness of the time, place, and emotional conditions we're in.

The same way traveling to a new place gives us greater understanding of the world if we truly open ourselves to the ways of that place, spirit offers us signs with valuable meaning—oftentimes as pure perspective without words—that we'll partake in much more fully through spirit's rich, layered languages. Consider this variety of languages through which spirit reaches us energetically with what we most need to receive:

1. VERBAL AND WRITTEN LANGUAGE . To start with the obvious, spoken and written language holds a wealth of ways for spirit to convey very specific messages to us. From our personal associations with individual letters to the many nuances in a phrase, a play on words, or a poetic sentence, the possibilities for both direct interpretation and symbolic inference are endless. Whether our gaze turns just in time to catch sight of giant words on a billboard telling us exactly what we need to hear when we're at a crossroads in life, or we "hear" the whisper of a beloved name through clairaudience without seeing anyone around who said it, verbal

and written language captures our attention so efficiently. Of course, an unfamiliar language's endless nuances also leave us wondering at times, as my time in Italy taught me, requiring us to engage our full body-mind-spirit apparatus in the interpretation.

To aid that interpretation, each of us is working from a distinct relationship with language that is both innate and learned. Anyone with synesthesia—the cognitive phenomenon that provokes a sense that is not the stimulated one, such as "hearing" a certain color with the tone of a musical note, or perceiving numbers and letters of the alphabet as specifically gendered—can attest to the layered ways we interpret language. The longer I've done spirit sessions with clients and experienced the multilayered quality of my most accurately sensed readings, I've suspected there must be a connection between my having synesthesia since before I can remember and my natural comfort with interpreting spirit energy. Any communication shorthand we use has a similar effect, like when close siblings or best friends can use a single word or even a small gesture to convey every detail of a shared story. The more significance we pull from any given symbol, the more extensive content we can receive through our capacity for shorthand. If verbal or written language isn't your most natural device for picking up detailed meanings, you're sure to have your own strong associations through one of the other following spirit "languages."

2. EMOTIONAL LANGUAGE. This one is for you highly sensitive empaths out there who thankfully have become a mainstream hot topic in recent years, as academic research and social media alike have flooded the world with content to better understand and appreciate your communication abilities. In terms of the spirit-sense tools, clairsentience is a strong gift for you. Through the complex language of emotions, divine energy can convey an enormous range of details about our lives and relationships. While

emotional language may seem entirely subjective and far more difficult to believe with certainty in our interpretation, anyone who is keenly empathic would point out that they often know the truth of a situation through its emotional subtext long before others relying on more overt communication pick up on it.

One mark of the quiet power of emotional language is that emotional content is apt to illicit physical responses in our bodies as well, from a gentle prickly sensation in the scalp to a stabbing pain in the heart. This physical punctuation helps to reinforce our specific interpretation of an emotion-based spiritual sign, usually with easily associated meanings. Learning about the body's seven energy centers—chakras in the yogic tradition—is a good place to start making meaningful connections between what's happening in your body and the emotional messages spirit is conveying to and through you. An emotional scale—a diagram easily found online that displays a detailed range of emotions from extremely low feelings like grief, depression, and hopelessness at one end to powerfully positive emotions like elation, love, and trust at the other end—is a valuable visual tool to focus your awareness on both the language of emotions and the physical sensations you associate with them. A clear signal that the spirit energy you're experiencing is flowing with divine perspective rather than an energy of lower vibration is that the emotional content coming from it is on the positive end of that emotional scale. When you're picking up sadness, anger, or angst through your clairsentience, that spiritual energy is informing you of an earthly human experience rather than a divine truth. Every human being, whether innately sensitive and empathic or not, can become more fluent in emotional language to understand the signs spirit is conveying— and, just as vitally, to understand our fellow living creatures.

3. MUSICAL LANGUAGE. Right up there with our speaking and our emotions on the list of distinctly complex human traits is our innate musicality, and it is a favorite language for spirit to reach us with through meaning beyond words. You may consider yourself categorically unmusical as far as your talents and interests go, but research reveals that even you were born with a shared language of patterns for exploring your environment, bridging connections with others, and—perhaps most fundamentally and vitally—expressing the rhythmic energy of your brain through music and its close partner, dance.[8] The vibrational variation of music provides an ideal platform for spirit energy, also vibrationally variable, to inhabit and evoke the messages our souls need, which our active minds might be closed to receiving.

Just as emotional language resonates through us physically, music, from the most primitive to the most elaborate, sends energetic details through our bodies to elicit understanding free of conscious thought. (Knowing how hard some of us try in meditation or exercise to release conscious thought for the sake of divine awareness, I find it touching to know how many other natural, delightful pathways divine spirit uses to offer itself for our recognition!)

TRY THIS: In a quiet space you have to yourself, play one of your favorite songs. Then turn off the music and be still in silence (with your eyes closed if you find that easier for tuning in to your body and awareness). What qualities of the song are left in and around you? A certain lyric? The line of notes strung together just right, forming that opening musical phrase you instantly recognize? The catchy rhythm? Or is it a vivid memory from the time you first fell in love with that song? A mental association you connect with its performers? Next, do the same thing with an entirely

8 Malloch, Stephen, and Colwyn Trevarthen, "The Human Nature of Music," *Frontiers in Psychology*, no. 9 (October 2018), https://doi.org/10.3389/fpsyg.2018.01680.

different song, ideally choosing one you don't know in a new genre with a new performer and different instruments. Notice what remains in the space and within your spiritual senses after the song this time. If you tune in to the subtle messages of your body and mind, I'd venture to bet that there's a lot more meaning resonating within you than you might have guessed, even though the song was unknown to you before.

This exercise doesn't have right or wrong answers so much as it demonstrates how easily you access meaningful interpretations through music. Something similar happens when we've spent time with another person or watched a movie. There is an unspoken language in the details of the exchange that affects and remains with us as mood-shifting, eye-opening content. It is that invisible, indescribable information that spirit communicates universally. The subtlety—the quiet voice of spirit that's always speaking when we pay attention—is why it's so important to be willing to alter our learned, literal mindset just a bit to engage with it. Feeling the essence of a song is the perfect practice for using your tools of spiritual language to grasp the messages within and just beyond the words, images, emotions, and yes, musical tunes, of the signs all around you.

4. ARTISTIC (AESTHETIC) LANGUAGE.   Just next door to musical language is another abundant source of messages from spirit energy: the aesthetic language of art, both intentional and seemingly accidental. Sort of a visual counterpart to music's use of sound patterns to communicate, artistic language can emanate from anything from a seashell's perfect spiral design—by the most mysterious, clever, and divine artist of all, Mother Nature—to a modern painter's impressionist rendering of a street scene. The old saying "Beauty is in the eye of the beholder" hints that we interpret art entirely from our own unique perspective, and yet we're also all participants in universal awareness whether we acknowledge

it or not, so universal themes and archetypes also play a subtle but powerful role in our interpretation of meaning through art. (Each of these favorite languages of spirit has its own divine way of connecting us intimately to something larger than ourselves. I'm convinced that is one of the greatest roles that spirit plays.)

It takes only a lesson or two in studio art to appreciate the energy and focus it takes to create a compelling artistic work. I watched my daughter, Anabel, train and practice in her art form—costume design for theater—for years and years to become a working professional artist out of college, which meant I also witnessed up close the giant dose of love it involves. Long before she got the chance to study design and production in a great university drama program, she was a four-year-old kid who created elaborate theatrical scenes out of the furniture, stuffed animals, and dress-up clothes in her bedroom before anyone else in the house had opened their eyes in the morning. In high school she spent her afternoons designing in the school's basement costume shop and her weekends creating collages and paintings as affectionate gifts or righteous political statements. Aesthetic language has been Anabel's daily mode of communication her whole life— so even though she is a young artist, I trust her fluent interpretation.

"Good artists are experts at making connections with and for the people who will take in their art," she pointed out to me recently. "It's an instinct for the different meanings viewers might take from their work. They're astute observers of people, of the world, and they don't need words to show it." With this insight, she also precisely described the way divine spirit presence observes us and the world. Like an artist with an instinct for just the right use of colors, empty spaces, and light and dark, divine wisdom in its comprehensive awareness uses such minute details to convey big meaning.

5. MATHEMATICAL LANGUAGE. No matter how much you either liked or despised math class as a kid, you must've been at least a little awestruck watching a natural math whiz hammer out a wall-size solution in a movie like *Hidden Figures* or *The Imitation Game*, or perhaps been confounded by the enormity of the calculus required to explain the movement and relationships of our solar system. Personally, what gets me the most giddy about mathematical language is how quickly it becomes obvious that it's as intertwined with the languages of art and music as they are with each other. No close inspection of any aspect of our universe—the one that surrounds us or the one within each of us—is complete without these diverse forms of expression bumping into and melding with each other constantly.

For example, take that seashell's spiral I mentioned earlier: it has a particular aesthetic appeal to our eye that mathematical language describes with a different precision than the artistic energy offers. Tracing back to the Greeks at the building of the Parthenon or even earlier to the Great Pyramid of Giza (and who knows how many unsung creations before and since), countless human-made and natural objects we perpetually consider aesthetically pleasing turn out to demonstrate what's known as the golden ratio or divine proportion. You may find this mathematical relationship in the dimensions of a shell as well as in a beautiful stained-glass window. Most of us may not take in the fact that the object's related components (graduating segments of shell spiral, for example) have a ratio equal to the ratio of their sum to the larger of the two parts. But that ratio is there, repeating in innumerable artworks, structures, and natural wonders. Similarly in music, except for the most avant-garde and purposefully unstructured pieces, precise fractions of time and space are the foundation of both the rhythmic and tonal qualities of what we hear.

What could be a more divine playground for spirit to reach us with complex meanings that will reverberate through us with great specificity than this mathematical language that abounds in everything around us?

6. NATURE'S LANGUAGE. Speaking of everything around us, the language of nature itself seems to take all these other energetic languages together as a complex and mysterious whole and show us what we need to know most universally through our lives. We receive silent signals through our emotional response to the changing quality of light indicating that a new season is beginning as naturally as our eyes tell us green leaves are beginning to sprout on branches. In our Western industrialized discourse, however, we might acknowledge the subtle language of nature as a useful tool for survival as it serves us in recognizing and avoiding danger, but we hamper ourselves severely by failing to celebrate and pass on the awareness of nature's essential, uplifting, and plainly instructive messages for well-being.

It's safe to say that in every spirit session with a client or larger group workshop, I end up speaking to the listeners' own life situations and personal power through at least one metaphor from nature. Most people come to this process of connecting with spirit from a place of needing to heal from something painful or from a longing to see major changes in their life, and the language of nature offers both soothing reassurance and stirring power through two broad categories of messages. First, the slow but consistent cycles of nature present a spiritual language landscape for us to understand the varying stages of our own lives, and second, nature's forces at work between objects' energy fields speak to us clearly about where our own quiet power lies. Whether the details of molecular physics or birds in flight are more apt to knock your socks off, nature's language is for all of us a birthright.

My favorite exchanges in this language usually happen in horseback riding. Not only can horses take us much farther than our own legs and lift us to a higher vantage point from which to take in the world, but the building of trust and unspoken collaboration between horse and rider have a way of dissolving all other questions and concerns. Having another being so willing and able to join you in communicating silently—for travel, discovery, or pure fun—is one of the greatest gifts to experience. Engaging in this partnership is a beautiful metaphor for our travel through life itself. For anyone who's never spent time on horseback, I usually describe the amazing way horse and rider agree on the direction and pace to move, which is through barely perceptible exchanges of energy. A horse senses where you expect him to go as soon as you shift the gaze of your eyes. In turn, I've found that subtlety of communication makes me more aware of the changes, desires, and goals happening within me energetically before they manifest more obviously on the outside. (I remember my driver's ed teacher pointing out the same mechanism in driving a car on a curvy highway and discovering he was right: if I traced the inside of each curve with my eyes, my control of the car was more fluid.) Using focus as an energetic tool to find dexterity through soft awareness instead of force is more than a lesson to learn from observing animals; it is our own natural power too, and it speaks to our potential in every aspect of our lives.

Each of these languages spirit speaks also conspire beautifully to answer a deep, dual desire you and I carry: to be seen and known in our unique specificity and to be in good company—not in spite of but instead due to being our true selves. Spirit reflects and joins us in any direction we turn our gaze, often when we're hardly aware we've chosen it.

The most supportive messages in a language most aligned with your detailed path will be abundantly available to you. As soon as you acknowledge the direction you want to go and fix your eyes, your focus, and your posture in that direction, you'll notice the conspiratorial energy increases. It's really Law of Attraction 101, which I don't explicitly teach or elaborate on in my practice but is beyond plentiful in popular sources everywhere these days as I mentioned in Chapter 2. And we are all talking about the same fundamental principles in our own different languages.

"Energy flows where attention goes," a shaman will tell you.

"Like attracts like," the physics teacher will say.

"To have a good friend, be a good friend," a life coach might counsel.

Are you starting to realize you have been multilingual all along? By recognizing the many different languages—energetic platforms, fields of understanding, areas of giftedness—through which you access your own spiritual nature, you're well on your way to being a more effective, intentional participant in that universal dance.

6

Systems: Find Spirit
in Collective Endeavors

We've spent much of this book in contemplation and observation of ourselves as individually gifted body-mind-spirit beings. Even though I've given you exercises to try that have included physical action in some cases, they've had a largely solitary, internalized focus for you to reorient yourself toward regularly noticing spirit energy, both within and immediately around you. Now we reach a sort of pivot point where we'll carry the internalized awareness from those earlier practices and turn back out into the shared reality of engaged, interactive daily life with others. Our aim is to begin noticing the many and varied systems of human living that are no less spirit-filled than our individual contemplative practices can be. In fact, I hope you'll end up finding some of your most powerful divine encounters happen in some of the most mundane, dare I say the profane, seemingly least sacred parts of your life as you interact and entangle with other people in the shared human systems of your life.

Even with this outward, worldly focus, you'll continue to observe and appreciate how your body's signals guide you and what your mind believes about the world around you, especially as you revisit your belief inventory from Chapter 2 to enlist that fluid power you have to expand in consciousness and belief through experience. Using those tools, we're about to shift energetic focus into what it is we're all doing here with each other on Earth every day, learning and working collectively to create systems that influence us personally and ultimately shape our ongoing human evolution.

TRY THIS: Before going further, give yourself a chance to connect directly with what I mean by "collective" energy. You're participating in a great web of interaction with everything else in the universe constantly and in too many ways to count. But in one of life's greatest mysteries, you're able to maintain an illusion of separateness, of individuality, to get through your day efficiently. That's not necessarily a bad thing; efficiency is meaningful, but we should remember it's sometimes much better achieved by collaborating with something bigger than our individual selves.

So what does returning your inner awareness to collective energy feel like? I'm going to ask you to recall middle school sleepovers for this one. If you didn't have a lot of sleepovers with groups of friends at that time, it's OK—I'll tell you about one of mine. It was sixth grade, and about six of us were over at Sarah's house for her birthday overnight. After all the pizza eating and running around her yard we could take, someone suggested we play "Light as a feather, stiff as a board." If you don't know it, the name of the game is a mantra. Energetically it works just like a mantra your yoga teacher instructs you to use in meditation, and in the case of this game, all the participants repeat it over and over together while circled in a squat around one person who is lying in the middle, completely still. While we all repeated, in unison, "Light as a feather, stiff as a board. Light as a feather, stiff as a board," the tallest and heaviest friend in the group,

Ashley, lay on the ground with her eyes closed and silently joined us in the mantra. The rest of us held out two fingers of each hand under Ashley, and somehow using eye contact for timing and never breaking our slow and steady mantra, the other five of us lifted Ashley nearly to the low ceiling of Sarah's upstairs bedroom. As soon as our wide-eyed amazement turned to giggling and shrieks, the "spell" was broken and she came tumbling down in a heap with us cushioning her fall the best we could.

You may want to play this game with your friends, but you can also try out this concept with as few as one or two other people and a heavy item like a sack of gardening soil, for example, or anything that seems impossible to pick up with only two fingers and the companions at hand. Some things to keep in mind:

In the case of our sixth-grade sleepover, we were still at a pretty innocent age, willing to believe in possibilities. That fresh, credulous outlook is divine spirit energy that also contributes force toward the outcome the group intends. Even if you're not an innocent kid anymore, you can cultivate that mood and attitude before jumping in.

The participant in the middle who is embodying the light feather/ stiff board in the game is just as crucial a participant to the collective success of the lift. In our case, I know Ashley was all in, focused, believing, and repeating the mantra with us. If you're going to try this with an inanimate object, just know that you and each person in your group will need to be willing to communicate with it energetically, knowing it has all the fundamental properties needed to respond to your energy too.

The piece of this exercise that is both a requirement and a lesson is, don't simply try the way you're used to doing something in order to achieve the desired effect. Every participant needs to trust the collective energy to do the work. Each individual's work is internal. Trust and focus are the job of your body-mind-spirit apparatus we attended to in Part I of this book. Now it's time to see what it does in collaborative settings.

I have come to know that our systems—those group endeavors, projects, institutions, and organized actions we take with others—are also platforms for divine spirit to show itself as a productive force. In those ventures where our human will and creativity have come together with those of others and begun to build something, our human divinity becomes concrete. Let's talk about how spirit shows up there, in those marvels of divine action here on the ground, so that you'll begin to become an expert at enlisting divine spirit energy where you care most about results. That's real-life awesome power.

Systems for Every Soul

I use the label "systems" for the most impromptu, unintentional displays of collective spirit energy as well as for the more sophisticated, highly organized efforts, whether they're as simple as two people stepping forward to help an elderly person up the stairs or as massive as the construction of a skyscraper. What these examples have in common is their demonstration of how an individual's greater power grows the more that person focuses their time, attention, effort, practice, heart, and ideally goodwill into a particular expression of their own gifts and then combines that accumulated positive energy with others' complementary efforts that are also born out of their individual soul's devoted focus.

A clarinetist has studied, practiced, and honed the ability to play a specific instrument over the course of many years before coming together with others who've been working with their own clarinets, then joining percussionists, violinists, flautists, and other musicians to play a complex composition, which, in many cases, someone unknown personally to all of them imagined and put to paper hundreds of years prior to the achievement realized by this marvelous system, the orchestra. Their performance comes together as an even larger collective success when the audience who gathers to witness it feels inspired by the spirit energy coursing through the music. In another field entirely, the person who has studied nearly every branch of science, sat for countless exams, practiced, and studied even more to become a competent surgeon goes into an operation not only with her own intention and skill but as part of a collective energy stream that is the modern medical system. Centuries of scientific discovery, trial and error by physicians long gone, and the devoted trust of history's billions of patients are all present energetically in the collegial work of the surgical team of individuals performing the life-affirming procedure of the moment (not to mention all of the other energy that built the hospital and equipment they use).

If you don't see a bit of divine spirit at work in such shared human feats, look again. The divine part of our nature especially relishes this kind of slowly built, carefully practiced, devotedly executed endeavor. In fact, you'll probably agree that everything that genuinely moves us to the reverence we previously learned to seek out has those characteristics. And in our present world that has swung vigorously toward favoring instant gratification, automation, and fifteen-second bits of social influence, it is essential to lift up and revere long-built, complex systems for the glorious expressions of collective divine spirit that they are.

1. THE FAMILY. Everyone's earliest experience of a collective system is the family. In whatever size and form it takes, composed of the

people we are born to and the people we grow up with (even if they're different people), this system has formative power in our lives. We know their influence is strong from many different academic fields that focus entire bodies of research on the details of family systems, from genetics to generational trauma.

And what does the soul-path, spirit-level perspective say about the family system? The family may be an even stronger force than any scientist, social or biological, has fully explained. In the hundreds of spirit readings I've done, every one has called forward at least one family member, and nearly always someone from more than one generation past in the listener's heritage, reminding each person that their lived experience is part of a much larger story web. Even in cases where a client was adopted or had never known the spirit person in life because they had died before the client was born, everyone has a spirit energy presence pointed toward them with special interest, care, protection, and hope for the potential healing and expansion of the family line. Remember Clara's story about the grandmother who hadn't raised Clara's father but communicated the specific advice for Clara to seek healing through saltwater? You have a family member—possibly a grandmother, great-great uncle, cousin twice removed, or yes, even a child lost early in their physical life—whose ever-present spirit is attentive to your highest good too.

The complex emotional learning ground of a family, on which both painful and supportive interactions help form our orientation toward new experiences, does not end, according to what I have witnessed in spirit sessions. Its fertile land spreads and enriches with each life that joins the system, each soul member's individual will for well-being and self-expression adding energy to the whole. The trauma within that system also travels throughout and can show up in any member's energy, in both directions past and future through generations, until the healing and well-being of a particular member overcomes it for them all. I continually receive spirit messages of gratitude for a living relative's influence on the energetic healing of people whose physical lives ended long before. This power elevates the prospect and potential of family therapy, doesn't it?

2. THE NEIGHBORHOOD. I include in this category of spiritual system much more than the five or six square blocks around whatever place you call home, but I choose the word "neighborhood" over "community" for its intimacy. We may be able to distance ourselves a bit physically or intellectually from someone who's part of our community, but a more closely bound "neighbor" reflects divine spirit's view of our true interconnectedness with each other. If you're a student or teacher, your school system is one of your neighborhoods (and also plays a role in your governing system, which we'll get to next). A regular support group like AA or even a book club could be a spiritual neighborhood system. Any shared, collective energy experience with intimate connection to your day-to-day life and growth (outside of your family) would be a spiritual neighborhood in the sense that your soul has close contact and mutual influence with the other souls who participate in it.

The degree of personal investment is fairly equal for neighborhood members—though different in quality from person to person—similar to a family system. Even an intimate romantic relationship, about which I might fill an entirely separate book to map its spiritual complexity and power, is a neighborhood system to spirit. While some of us end up considering our best friends and beloved partners our family, these systems have an entirely distinct role and energy from that of a family lineage and present differently to an intuitive reader. Whereas a family system's collective energy went into the actual cell formation within our bodies where our soul's energy joined with theirs, in a neighborhood system, the energetic influence is external and, though valuable and necessary for our growth, effectively optional.

How then would a collective energy system we're able to opt out of have such a powerful role in our lives? If we don't have to be part of that shared experience of eating at the same corner diner for breakfast every Saturday alongside the same locals sharing the counter week to week, why do we feel quietly compelled to be there? Especially if the fellow diners are curmudgeons, or the coffee is terrible? The answers are specific to each soul participating in a neighborhood system, but they always have something to do with the path of growth each person is on. Sometimes the people who come to me for spirit readings are surprised I pick up messages about a system like that before seeing a connection of theirs that is more emotionally intense, such as a romance. Once we enlist the perspective of spirit, the lessons are clear and beneficial to the listener's ability to wake up to some aspect of their soul's power in this life.

Consider an actual next-door neighbor you've had—a close one, preferably, maybe even someone with whom you've shared common walls in an apartment building or dorm. Unless you've been extra lucky, a neighbor usually rubs us the wrong way on at least a couple of topics. They practice the drums too loudly (hard not to mention this example, as it's happening out my window as I write this), they park their car five inches too close to yours, they're a family of yellers, they order endless packages and leave them out on the step. We judge our neighbors. We envy our neighbors. According to the Bible's Old Testament, the risk of coveting our neighbors' possessions and wives was common enough to warrant its own commandment. Neighbors, in other words, are the people in our lives who test our character, our souls' alignment, and our self-awareness. Any neighborhood system is a potential learning ground.

3. THE GOVERNING BODY. Take the pervasive nature of a family system's spiritual influence and mix in some of a neighborhood system's challenging energy, and you find the vibrational realm of a governing system. Depending on where we happened to be born, the structure of our government may include layers that seem to have little direct effect on our daily experience. However, every aspect of the history, intention, and method infused in our lifestyles settles within our being like environmental residue. Potentially benevolent, possibly violent, sometimes protective, corrupt, equalizing, polarizing, or neglectful, a governing system's spiritual energy holds many facets, and the way we individually engage with them differs depending on our unique body-mind-spirit focus.

We know anecdotally that, violent revolution aside, significant change in a governing system occurs extremely slowly. It's hardly a wonder, considering this shared system includes so many different participants' energies and all the history it took to build it. Wars, migration, colonization, natural disasters, political discourse on millions of topics, they all stay within the collective system as energy. The aspects that align more closely with divine energy help propel all participants forward positively, and the destructive or simply misaligned elements ultimately drag all participants down as a collective. Certainly anecdotes also tell us that plenty of individuals appear to thrive on the surface in corrupt systems too, but just as a powerful hurricane or an earthquake spares no one, the effects of negative energy on the whole do find their way to everyone in some way or other.

Unless, as in a family system, some of the shared trauma or discord built into a governing system is healed. The most dramatic example I've seen from afar during my life was the collective agreement in South Africa to establish a Truth and Reconciliation Commission to heal the effects of violent apartheid against black citizens. When I was a kid, Cape Town's archbishop and Nobel Peace Prize winner Desmond Tutu visited my church in California on occasion and spoke in his gorgeous, divine-on-earth voice of our collective engagement in all systems, down to the very fact of being human. "My humanity is caught up in yours," he often said, and he spent his life teaching and reteaching that principle to some powerful healing effects in his country and others. In North America, our work in truth and reconciliation over the centuries of violent oppression of Indigenous peoples and black Americans will be a similarly long process—not to erase the accumulated negative energy of the past, which is energetically residual in all of us still participating in the system, but to acknowledge and overcome it with a collective healing focus.

4. THE PHYSICAL INFRASTRUCTURE. Within and connected to one of the other larger systems (family, neighborhood, or government), the physical structures that support our day-to-day life all hold shared spiritual energy as well. Whether engaged in big-city dwelling or a simple rural existence, every earthly life happens within multiple infrastructure systems. From the minute details of a shared bed, the physical arrangement of a whole room, or the tidiness of a house to the more complex energies of a whole block of buildings, road features, and shared spaces like parks or commercial districts, the infrastructure around you has an interactive effect with your energy and the others who use it. An example of the subtle but strong power of these systems is the effect on children attending a school that's in a state of disrepair and unsanitary conditions. Ample evidence, even lawsuits, over the psychological and physical dangers to both students and teachers spending their days in such buildings points scientifically to the role of infrastructure, and our growing awareness of the spiritual energy in every person, object, and interaction supports those findings from yet another essential perspective. Looking at a problem like underperforming

schools through a holistic lens that takes the collective energy system into account can lead to solutions when we recognize we all share in the effects.

TRY THIS: To experiment using your body-mind-spirit relationship with infrastructure systems, the Chinese practice of feng shui provides beautiful clarity. Making use of the varied energetic qualities of the five elements of earth, fire, water, wood, and metal, feng shui is a way to cultivate certain energy in your space to support a certain mood or reach a goal. Along with teaching how the qualities of those elements interact with our own energy, the practice employs them through specific placement in relation to each other within a room to have a collective, repetitive effect on us.

Choose a small sample of your personal infrastructure where you spend a lot of functional time—perhaps the desk where you work, your kitchen, or your car. This experiment is a good time to bring out your journal to make a few "before" notes about the part of your life that the infrastructure supports and its current state. For example, "My car serves me by transporting me to and from my workplace every day. It has a broken door handle on one side, food containers on the floor, and a 'Check Engine' warning light on display. The seats are sandy from my weekend trips to the beach, which I love for the escape. I don't use the trunk of my car because it is full of clothes I need to take to Goodwill."

Make as many simple changes to declutter that part of your infrastructure as you can. Remove and discard or repurpose anything in the space that doesn't serve you anymore, such as cooking tools missing a handle, old earbuds you never use, or clothes that don't fit. Thank them for their service and let them go. Thoroughly clean the area and arrange the few remaining items in an orderly way that supports your easy access and use of them. In the example of the car, you'd make the time to have the engine checked and even thoroughly vacuum all of that beach sand that makes you think of escape when you need to be present for a workday. (Don't worry; there will be more sand waiting for you at the beach.) Make sure the changes you make to the small infrastructure are noticeable in the greater ease and flow they support while you're using it.

After a week, return to the journal and describe the space or room again, along with any notable experiences in your mood or achievements. Have you noticed that you're catching more green lights on your commute? Are you getting along better with your office mates? Did you meet an incredible lifeguard on your weekend beach trip? You get the idea. The energy of the spaces and the tools we use follow us wherever we go. Improving one small portion of your life can have surprising results in ways you wouldn't expect. Everything is interconnected. If you're inspired to see even more powerful results, feng shui offers many more specific details for improving the flow of energy in your life. Find an online resource or book you like about the practice and keep experimenting with it. The exploration may lead you to discover how good you feel surrounded by modern architecture, or how productive you are if you start each day with a walk beside your town's river. These details of our infrastructure offer another level on which to know ourselves within the collective and to see the quality our lives can take on through intentional interaction with spirit energy.

5. THE SPECIALIZED PURSUIT.   In many examples in this book, you'll notice one of my favorite sources of inspiration for cultivating reverence is the variety of specialized pursuits that human beings choose to immerse themselves in collectively with others. The jazz ensemble, the synchronized swim team, and the crew behind the scenes on a movie set are all examples; anywhere people are devoting

their full body, mind, and spirit to an endeavor in coordination with others offers a chance to witness divine nature at work in vivid color.

The outcome of the collective pursuit doesn't need to be your cup of tea in order for you to appreciate the phenomenon you're witnessing. Over many months last year I became a devoted viewer of a TV docuseries about Formula 1 car racing. Granted, I started watching to bond with my teenage son during a time when his life was naturally taking him further and further away from hanging out with Mom, but while it was his idea to start the show, I ended up being the one to ask him to watch it with me. The extent of the collective effort, time, practice, athletic training, dedication, and passion I found absolutely surging through the F1 world (and yes, even the money) truly stirred my soul as if I were participating in one of my own personal interests, which I can't say race cars ever had been. Of course it is fairly inconsequential to be interested in car racing or not. The point is that our shared human experience offers such abundance and variety that it can thrill us if we see it for what is really going on. Each participant is a miracle machine on their own, and when shared inspiration flows through a lot of us at once, the most exciting things happen.

In considering the systems of specialized pursuits you encounter, keep in mind the universe is big enough for all of them. No single specialized pursuit is more important than the others, even if we try to identify a moral superiority in one or a pointless quality in another (destructive, unjust occupations excluded). The individuals within their own world of focus very different from yours arrived at their pursuit through a complex, unique mix of energies and layers upon layers of collective systems, which serve more purposes than your eye can see.

Don's Story: The Power of Collaboration

Don is dad to some of my best childhood friends, and he is a connector. You might know people who are connectors: individuals who seem to know a million other people and have a way of facilitating new friendships, partnerships, projects, and joint endeavors. Professionally he is a physician, and he was head of the emergency room at our city's biggest hospital when I was a kid. As I've mentioned, I grew up in an intellectual, highly educated community, and I was surrounded by successful leaders in traditional fields like business, medicine, law, and—thanks to our local NASA Jet Propulsion Laboratory and Caltech—science and technology. The collective focus of energy toward the exceptional, high-stakes pursuit of knowledge was and is strong in my hometown of Pasadena. And once you're in that vibrational realm, collective expectations are high for all of the community's systems to flow well. Don is a facilitator of exceptional results like that.

All this put him in just the right place at the right time when inevitable symptoms of misalignment in the larger systems of governing and infrastructure appeared at home, as they eventually do everywhere. California statistics in the 1980s revealed an alarming number of local children were living in families with no health insurance—and with the costs of medical care growing, that meant a lot of kids weren't going to the doctor or dentist, even when they greatly needed one.[9] As these systemic ailments do in the United States even today, the lack of health care most acutely affected children of Latino and black families of lesser economic means. It was a city replete with physicians (I know because practically

9 Spiegel, Clair, "Uninsured Children Pay Price: Millions are not covered because their parents cannot afford policies. Simple medical problems go untreated and often lead to serious illness and tax the health care system," *Los Angeles Times*, June 23, 1992, https://www.latimes.com/archives/la-xpm-1992-06-23-mn-1058-story.html.

every other kid at my school had a parent called "Doctor"), but thousands of kids weren't getting care.

Knowing the human body's interconnecting systems thoroughly, Don understood that the whole cannot be well if a part is sick. (We can all understand the ripple effects on the whole of society when too many children are left sick.) And since he is extremely compassionate, the kids on their own would have been motivation enough for him, but his ability to see the interaction of systems—people, organizations, governing practices, environmental circumstances—led him to a solution.

While Don's youngest daughters and I were teenagers, focused on friends and our futures, I was aware through parents' conversations that Don had begun enlisting his fellow physicians around Pasadena to see a couple of young patients for free every month. As he saw it, those free appointments would be a relatively minor contribution for an individual doctor to provide, but added together, they could make a huge dent in the seemingly intractable health care woes of families in the city.

Now decades later, Young & Healthy is a renowned nonprofit organization with its roots in Don's idea for collaboration. More than 350 medical professionals, 500 community volunteers, and hundreds of partnering organizations participate in providing health services to the area's children and families who need them. Even in Pasadena's "exceptional" intellectual environment, at least 60 percent of kids in its public schools experience poverty.[10] But now that a long-built system of compassion, skill, and medical knowledge has grown from collective energetic focus toward their well-being, they have access to a healthier start in life.

---

10 "Students Eligible for Free or Reduced Price School Meals," KidsData.org, Population Reference Bureau, https://www.kidsdata.org/topic/518/school-meals/table#fmt=675&l oc=2,127,347,1763,331,348,336,171,321,345&tf=141&sortType=asc.

Disrupting Collective Energy Is Divine Too

When you consider how often systems go awry under human influence or nature's cycles of growth and deterioration, we do need to recognize the value of disruptors. Physical life includes changes, no matter what we actively do to influence them. Sometimes I notice the hidden divine quality of a destructive event and have to laugh at how often we humans tend to kick and scream over those forces that may seem to hurt in one way but clearly open the door for new life in another. We are not exempt from the destruction those complex interactions of the universe's systems sometimes bring. As soon as we accept that fact of nature, it is even possible to cultivate destructive change itself as an intentional, powerful tool.

I've recently noticed some moments in sacred ceremonies in which our instinct to appreciate the divinity of disruption is apparent. After Queen Elizabeth II of England died, I saw a clip of the extremely formal and traditional funeral rites the Church of England used to mark her departure from Earth. Much of the music and ceremony was familiar to me, since I grew up in the American Episcopal Church, which has its roots in the Anglican tradition, but I had never seen anything like the lord chamberlain breaking a stick over her coffin and laying the broken pieces on top. Symbolizing the end of his decades of duty to the queen as her primary steward, the moment stood out from the otherwise predictable service. It reminded me of an entirely different tradition in Jewish weddings, when the newly married groom smashes glass on the floor by stomping on it. With this tradition the action is a remembrance of the destruction of the Jewish temples, and its interweaving into a moment of joyful celebration reminds those gathered not to get too comfortable in joy or in sorrow. Life flows with both.

When you notice a disruptor in your world—the guy breaking all the traffic rules and driving you crazy on the freeway, a student in your class who always does the opposite of what you've asked, or a neighbor practicing the drums, a little offbeat and very loudly just outside your window, remember that the divine in us asks for disruption at times too. We become stronger as a result and more ready to participate in the collective, our full selves engaged.

Part III

Active Engagement of Spirit

Part III

7

Traditional Channels: Work with What You Have

In this second half of the book, I want to help you jump all the way in—with your grounded, earthly life very much intact—to use with intention your awareness of spirit all around and in you. This will make your life the rich wonder of daily divinity it was meant to be when you landed here. By now you know that by "daily divinity" I don't mean constant utter joy or booming-voice-of-God revelations like you might see in a Sunday school video. I'm talking about a sense of your own wholeness, power, and readiness. And please, yes, delight in this earthly experience.

These days, the goal of a truly uplifted spirit may not jibe with the concept you have of organized religion and spiritual traditions. The harmful results of extremism have dominated the news and our public conversation about religion for decades now, leaving so many of us to want to disassociate ourselves from anything that hints of established religion or even secular social traditions. But I'm going to suggest we not throw the baby out with the bathwater on religion and established traditions. Certain aspects of the divine still reside most abundantly in religious practices, and some of the more traditional parts of our mainstream life do actually hold abundant potential for your engagement with spirit. You can trust yourself to make just as good use of tools that are old and worn by many hands as you do the personal ones that belong to you alone.

Millennia of Religious History Don't Lie

It is much more likely that your grandparents made religious practices a priority in their lives than that you do. Not just in the United States but across the globe, trends in the last two decades have told us that religion is on its way out as industrialized, secularized society no longer finds it useful. Between 2007 and 2019, data in forty-three of forty-nine countries around the world supported that fact.[11] Yet there's no denying we still feel an inner call toward a spiritual life. (I mean, you're reading this book.) Somehow winging it the whole way, without guidance, and keeping it entirely to ourselves in private doesn't quite satisfy that spiritual longing, so we may join support groups, workshops, or full moon ceremonies. Even those who wouldn't be caught dead near anything labeled spiritual join teams, follow rituals, and put up symbols of meaning. Why not acknowledge that since the beginning of recorded history and likely starting much, much earlier, human beings have naturally been religious for good reason? Trends aside, there are valuable qualities unique to religion and practiced social traditions that serve our direct connection to spirit.

First of all, let's clear away some of the clutter surrounding religion today and take a more anthropological view of it, as a human behavior

---

11 Inglehart, Ronald, Jon Miller, Michael Dennis, Stephanie Jwo, and Gergely Rosta, "Religion's Sudden Decline, Revisited," University of Michigan Institute for Social Research, Center for Political Studies, February 26, 2021, https://cps.isr.umich.edu/news/religions-sudden-decline-revisited/.

with natural origins and cultural purpose. At present we're caught up in a difficult era of transition beyond the world-dominating white patriarchal power structure, which means the religions that rely on a presupposition of male authority are an endangered species. We also know from human history that they're not the only kind of organized spirituality humans know how to form, and it may well be that we remember that in our DNA. Whatever your (dis)comfort level is with that change, it is clearly underway and will take a very long time, so don't let that fight bog down your natural-born access to the divine right here and now.

How do some of these practices, which most established traditions and religions share, apply to you?

1. SHARED COSMOLOGY. Nope, this practice doesn't mean going to the same hair stylist as your friends. (That one was for my grandpa.) It doesn't necessarily have to be as out there as tracking the positions of the planets and stars to make major life decisions either. Our cosmology is simply our sense of ourselves within the larger whole, whatever we see that whole to be. How does this universe I'm in relate to me directly, and what's my role in it? It's the set of questions we all end up asking at some stage, whether silently or very publicly, and usually over the course of childhood and adolescence, we move from wide-eyed wonder into more fixed ideas about the answers. That process often has a lot to do with the collective energy systems we talked about in the previous chapter. We absorb the practices of our families, schools, and other influential systems around us to learn what our individual lives mean.

You can laugh, but I remember watching the animated Disney film *Moana*—as a full-grown adult—with envy of the shared cosmology the title character absorbs through a tradition shared with her grandmother. While Moana is surrounded by islanders who believe tending their own land and shoreline is the extent of their place and role in the universe, her grandmother shares a personal outlook with her about feeling a little different from the family and community. She embodies that perspective in her daily practice of "dancing with the waves" and invites Moana to join her in the ritual. The regularity of their joint celebration of a shared view of themselves in the universe prepares Moana spiritually for the tough adventures she undertakes at sea. Our complex lives are no children's movie, but the allegories these stories offer are obviously useful; otherwise so many adults wouldn't keep loving them alongside their kids. (If you watch and love them and don't even have kids, you're my kind of romantic soul.) In the same way, the shared stories on which a religion is built provide a structure in which to interpret our own lives and purpose for being.

Religious practice can be as simple as the daily ritual of dancing in reverence toward the ocean, as Moana's grandmother does. Do you have a daily or weekly routine to acknowledge your cosmology and those you share it with? I have a friend who adores the cycles of the moon, and nearly every month she sends me a text with a description of the spiritual characteristics of the full moon about to appear. The text may arrive when I'm in the middle of a chaotic grocery store or hyper-focused on a workshop outline, and each time, I try to pause and absorb what it says as soon as she sends it. The sharing itself is a big part of the gift of this intentional connection to spirit. In these notes my friend is giving me a figurative "namaste"—a greeting that in the yogic tradition means, in essence, "The divine in me recognizes the divine in you"—yet another way of sharing one's cosmology with others. Taking these examples, you'll likely come up with a version of outwardly acknowledging your role in the universe (that you already do or would be comfortable trying) in order to build a connection of cosmology with someone close to you.

2. REGULAR GATHERING. Habits of coming together with others for intentional soul-to-soul connection do not have to be religious to hold spiritual benefit. Certainly some people came to cherish the practice more after any gathering was effectively prohibited during a global pandemic, but it's hardly a given that everyone makes a habit of gathering regularly in community anyway. In places where the culture emphasizes busyness and relies heavily on technology, we may let long stretches of time pass without connecting in person with a group in shared activity or purpose. A hefty portion of the United States isn't involved in any community group, whether for a social connection, volunteerism, professional association, hobby, or religious routine. That "zero involvement" figure was 43 percent in 2017, and post-pandemic, more than a third of Americans reported feeling social gatherings had become less important to them.[12] (Yet 97 percent of the US population has a cell phone, the tool that helps ensure we scarcely need to interact IRL.[13])

The word on regular social connection, from neuroscience to psychology to kitchen wisdom, is that human beings ultimately need social connection for survival, not just for kicks. I'd suggest this area of study is one of the best demonstrations of how intertwined our body, mind, and spirit are, and it tells us that spirit is not a part-time side gig to take care of when you have extra time. Our brains register social rejection the same way they do physical pain, so it stands to reason that loneliness has a direct correlation to inflammation in the body, cardiovascular health risks, and accelerated aging and early mortality.[14] And remember: from a

---

12 "CPS News," Center for Political Studies, February 26, 2021, https://cps.isr.umich.edu/news/religions-sudden-decline-revisited/.
13 "Mobile Fact Sheet," Pew Research Center: Internet, Science & Tech (Pew Research Center, November 16, 2022), https://www.pewresearch.org/internet/fact-sheet/mobile/.
14 Beckman, Mary, "Rejection Is Like Pain to the Brain," Science.org, American Association for the Advancement of Science (AAAS), October 9, 2003, https://www.science.org/content/article/rejection-pain-brain.

divine perspective of your soul's journey, it's the interaction with others in relationship that stretches you to expand and improve your knowledge of yourself.

Carefully choosing whom you'll gather with and for what purpose is the way to make even a secular activity with others bring you into closer connection with spirit. Belonging to a book club that always ends up tossing the book aside to gossip might be one source of interaction to put on pause because of its drag on your energy, while joining a small group of people who want to learn how to surf as much as you do has the potential to stimulate your body-mind-spirit apparatus and oneness with nature at the same time. You won't see many big spiritual breakthroughs until you create your own cracks in your status quo. It's OK to make them small cracks at first; the divine in and around you will help with the rest.

3. SEASONAL AND DAY-TO-DAY RITUALS. If you don't have much firsthand experience with an organized religion, you might not realize how specifically many of those traditions recognize and honor changes in time and season with their practices. For the Episcopal Church I grew up in (and other denominations of Christianity), the liturgical calendar provides detailed guidance for what parts of scripture are read each week of the year, what colors are used on the altar and priests' vestments, and any festivals that are celebrated for that period of the year. The Book of Common Prayer specifies sacred words to be used in rituals at different times of day, in rites to mark births and deaths, and even the way to pray for specific causes like a person's education or social justice in the world. Together with such sacred language that is passed down from generation to generation, ritual in a religious setting usually includes very specific order of movements, gestures, or placement of cherished symbolic objects. Adding a specific component that marks the passage of time or the natural turning of seasons helps provide

reliable reference points to the greater universe too (supporting that sense of cosmology). Even if all of it looks bizarre to an outsider looking in on a ritual, we can at least acknowledge the energetic quality of each of these intentional components and appreciate that the participants' practice is having an energetic effect on them that we may not see.

Ritual is a part of your life already in ways you don't necessarily consider spiritual (although I've heard people say things like "skiing is my church," so you may already be familiar with this concept). From making yourself a certain kind of tea every morning for a few minutes of silence before your family wakes up to sharing a secret handshake with your nephew every time you get together for family dinner, engaging in ritual is an instinctive human behavior. The goal in using this already-established part of your life for spirit connection is to incorporate some soul-feeding intention into it. Use the body-mind-spirit tools we explored in Part I of the book to notice how you're engaging with a ritual. Is there an aspect of it that feeds your sense of reverence? If your favorite ritual is getting together with your alumni club to drink beer at a football game, that too can be the perfect place to notice the elements of symbolism, specific language handed down through generations, and the gestures and practices that bond you with other souls. I'll say it again and again: an activity does not have to look "holy" or morally superior to hold powerful spirit energy that serves your soul's journey. You might be living a sacred life by accident.

TRY THIS: Consider your average week, and identify a ritual you follow most regularly. It can be as seemingly mundane as your stop at the drive-through Starbucks, a weekly FaceTime call with your brother in another state, or an organized meeting with coworkers. In your journal, keep a little record of the sacred elements you notice in that ritual. Does it help you mark your place in time, whether in the day or the larger calendar year?

Is there a set of specific motions your body makes or language that is part of the ritual every time? What treasured objects or symbols are included in the experience, and what meaning do they hold for you?

After simply keeping track of what you notice about the ritual a few times, consider whether it is providing you an access point to positive spirit energy or locking you in a more stagnant state. Your instincts and your journal notes will tell you whether there are small adjustments you can make (e.g., adding an intentional greeting to the way you speak to your Starbucks cashier or trading some simple words of benediction with your brother before signing off FaceTime) that will elevate the ritual and you along with it. Next, you'll commit to the spirit-lifting components of the ritual or create a new one and open up to the benefits it will bring you over time.

4. SPIRITUAL EXPERTS. Here is a very complex element of sacred tradition that can be so tangled in human fallibility (in the expert and the learner) that it becomes damaging rather than conducive to a direct connection with divine spirit. There have been too many people throughout history who've suffered trauma at the hands of a spiritual leader they've revered for me to skip mentioning the potential hazards of such a relationship. No person has a soul-level right to control, direct, spiritually punish, or change another. No one is born, nor divinely endorsed, to spiritually coerce or manipulate anyone else. One of the best arguments for developing your rich and powerful spiritual identity is to make it impossible to fall under that kind of control by another.

At the same time that we hold that awareness of toxic spiritual mentor–student scenarios, it's also possible to lift up and emulate wonderful examples of people who guide and propel us with their spiritual expertise. With the most transcendent of such spiritual experts, we experience them like a conduit or like a mirror—no more, and no less. (The best of these teachers have no personal stake in what's learned and neither veer past nor fall short of their purpose to others.) A conduit is one who channels divine energy to flow toward others in the form of insightful guidance, healing, or comfort. Think back to that magical nurse who looked after your child in the emergency room and calmed you whenever you watched her work, or the social activist who gave a speech on TV that physically jolted you to commit more deeply to a cause. These everyday people were conduits for the healing and wisdom of the divine, each in their own unique way. A mirror is someone who has done their own work in body, mind, and soul to the degree that they hold a still, beautiful balance of the three. They seem to effortlessly reflect back to others what their own souls long to achieve. Both forms of teaching are incredibly valuable gifts on your journey.

Whether a mentor appears in your life just once with exactly what you need in a moment (sometimes unwittingly) or they play a longer role over time, you can intentionally absorb the guidance of spirit through such a relationship. Using your own spiritual senses, you have the instinct and discernment to feel your way to understanding the nuggets of divine wisdom they offer that you need most. Regurgitating a mentor's guidance word for word is never the point. Elevating and praising them as more holy or valuable than you isn't either. By focusing on remaining grounded in the knowledge that you are also of divine energetic essence, you will be open to the new perspective and wisdom they offer while keeping your own gifts engaged.

5. SACRED OBJECTS . In my classes for people who want to explore the furthest reaches of their spiritual senses, we always have a session for trying out psychometry, which is the reading of energetic details

in objects. Taking the essential truths that everything is made of energy and energy is never created or destroyed but only changes form, we use our human gift for sensing energy and investigate the ability to translate the details it holds. The exercise is fun for everyone, because each person brings an object with distinct personal meaning and history and exchanges it with another student to try a psychometry reading on the other's treasure. The powerful, specific, and emotional information many participants pick up from the objects is astounding to everyone, and each item seems more sacred to the group in the end.

Were we to walk together into a museum, cathedral, mausoleum, or temple, the objects in those spaces might automatically earn our reverence. Culturally, we may associate sacred objects with religious tradition and accept them as such in those contexts without a lot of thought. I try to help students connect more intimately with the sacredness of objects through their own senses so that they discover they have access to the information to decide for themselves what they hold sacred.

Many of us remember a special object we had as a young child—a toy, a blanket, any odd bauble kids get attached to—that we were certain at the time had a life of its own. What makes someone leave behind the childhood sensitivity to the energetic life of an object? It's very important in the life of your spirit to make a distinction between childish and childlike tendencies. Children (ideally) have fewer demands on their time and mind space—unless they have an adult shoving an electronic device in their hands at every whimper—so their natural-born spirit senses have room to tune in keenly to the energy of people and things. That personal relationship with objects as holders of sacred details adds a layer of depth to our spiritual character and enhances our ability to hear the quiet, dancing voice of the divine everywhere.

Rick's Story: The Power of Community

Recently I sat across a restaurant table from my former therapist, Rick, the ferryman who had assisted me across murky waters into the unknown many years before, and I remembered why he was and still is the right spiritual mentor for me and many others in our community.

"So many people associate religion with guilt," Rick said between bites of his Caesar salad. "No one wants to think of themselves as doing something wrong. But what a religious community does is hold us accountable. If you're not held accountable by a community, it's so easy to get lost and lonely. I'm a product of that."

Before his years as a therapist, Rick was a Presbyterian minister and, as he tells it, "blew up his own life" decades ago when he was leading a quaint church with a beautiful family in an idyllic town close by. After a series of relationships with women outside the bounds of what his community and his own heart expected of him, all of the scaffolding that had been his daily life crumbled. He had to embark on a journey across murky waters that included a painful separation from his family, a hugely public scandal (think "long article in the Los Angeles Times published on Easter morning" kind of huge), and ejection from a career he loved. Rick is quick to state his culpability in this dismantling and also maintains that the church—the larger body of people with whom he shares a cosmology and a narrative of how the transcendent lives here on the ground level—played an essential role in his becoming whole again, even after his betrayal.

Rick recently wrote in an essay, "I had friends who loved my family and me through every day of the struggle we were in. They knew more than the public did about my indiscretions, and they were clear in their condemnation of my bad behavior. But their love for us and their acceptance of me as a deeply flawed but nonetheless redeemable human being ultimately outweighed the onslaught of judgment." He soon found himself in the embrace of another church (which happened to be the one I attended with my family from the time I was an awkward tween) with a new chance to use his gifts of spiritual teaching, which had not dissolved in his very human moments of failure.

The members of a religious community's ties to each other go much deeper than a shared activity. It's certainly possible for the members of a softball team to push each other to become better versions of themselves or for citizens of a small town to rally in support of a neighbor in trouble, but a community built on centuries-old spiritual traditions and rituals is (in many cases) purposefully tapped in to a universal energy aligned with healing and renewal. While the accountability infused with love that Rick experienced is not, unfortunately, how every religious community operates, many do hold some version of a shared view of every person as an individual expression of the divine, and they therefore remain supportive of each other through any lower energies they go through.

In a reinforcement of the faith he already had in his community, Rick saw the same fierce swell of love lift him and his family through unspeakable grief after the sudden death of one of his sons. Jesse was only twenty-four when he was killed in a vehicle accident while serving in the Peace Corps in Guinea, West Africa. (By this time, Rick and his wife had reunited and moved forward from the scandal that had crumbled their lives years before.) He told me, "For ten straight days after we got the news about Jesse, we didn't have to pick up a phone or lift a finger to feed ourselves." He listed the names of women I knew in our church community who had surrounded Rick's family with practical and emotional support, all with the kind of graceful intervention no one could know they want or need until they're in the middle of such a horrific ordeal.

When we were talking through his personal history with the church over lunch, Rick brought up a Bible story and barely had the words out before I jumped in to say it was my absolute favorite of the illustrated tales I remembered reading as a kid in Sunday school. Told in different ways in the three gospels of Matthew, Mark, and Luke, it recounts an occasion when Jesus was teaching a large gathering of people in a house in Capernaum, a fishing village on the Sea of Galilee. A group of men brought their paralyzed friend to the house in the hope that Jesus would heal him, but they couldn't get through the standing-room-only packed house with the man's stretcher. Undeterred, these men got up to the roof and made a hole through which they lowered their friend on his stretcher mat down into the room where Jesus was speaking. Rick's point in bringing up the story, it turned out, was to spotlight the same thing about it that had delighted me as a kid. It wasn't the part about Jesus performing a miracle that healed the man; it was the undeterred friends on the roof. Sometimes our best (or only) path to accessing that perpetual flow of powerful divine life force is discovered by trusting the divinity of our fellow human beings.

Whether or not you are able to reconcile with your reality the idea of a person healing another person in an instant—or in a girl next door picking up detailed messages from the energy of someone who's died—you have likely seen the power that a group of people with shared hope can have. We know that religious communities can be extremely flawed in approach or doctrine that drives people away instead of empowering them. And yet it does not preclude our appreciating the unique ways some religious practices support intentional connection with our shared divine spirit.

While I've been blessedly spared so far of the extreme experiences with excruciating loss like those my mentor Rick went through, I do know both self-inflicted suffering and the heartbreak of grief from unavoidable loss—and you surely do as well, because they are universal human experiences. If religion and other established spiritual traditions offer you anything on your journey of becoming aware of and engaged directly with spirit, let your takeaway be their purposeful calling in of divine energy in community and the rich relationships with other deeply engaged souls that process can foster.

8

Mystic Medium Mode:
Take a Wonder-Filled Journey

All right, let's put aside gently for a moment those traditions and structures to which the world has taught us to attribute all spiritual credibility and instead find it within ourselves. Are you ready to trust yourself as a spirit medium? Ready to connect directly with intention and channel valuable messages from other energy sources, whether from people in your world who've died, the angels or fairies you've wondered about, or even an animal spirit guide, like each student in one of my workshops eventually meets?

Yes. Let's say it together: you are ready. Each chapter so far has been preparing your body-mind-spirit apparatus to be powerful in a new way, and now it's time for a little direct lesson in mediumship!

Maybe what I've shared about my life and perspective hasn't quite matched what you've imagined about a psychic medium's world. If you have already started to see that a psychic medium could be any girl next door (or person at the bus stop or driver in the car next to yours), good. I've waited until this far into the book to give you specific guidance in how to connect as a spirit medium yourself with the hope that you'd get here with that perspective. You've realized by now that there is no such thing as a typical spirit medium—all of us have these abilities to some degree. When you understand through vivid firsthand experience the whole truth of spirit, from your earthly body on out to that expansive energy I call the divine, you come to understand that it's part of your everyday nature to be a channel for that energy. I offer all that preparation in Parts I and II because it is just plain easier to connect with spirit once one has that foundational understanding. And by now you're already most of the way there! You've been tuning in to spirit all along as you've made quiet connections using your body-mind-spirit apparatus to subtly take in those same invisible but powerful qualities in everything around you. The steady, daily practice of unifying all your natural tools into a collaborative whole pays off; it may have even startled you how well you can pick up accurate details through your spirit senses. The preparation you've been doing has been honing and lifting your energetic signature—the quality, color, and intensity of your spirit's light—to line you up with the most specific, fulfilling, and soul-expanding guidance for you on your path. And isn't that really the point?

A Word on the Drama of Spirit Connection

Well, OK—for some people, the point of all this spirit business is not purely uplifting but something more tantalizing. A lot of the questions I get, both in my work and in casual conversation, tell me that the intrigue of evil spirits, dark forces, and enigmatic cosmic destinies holds strong sway over many people. And I understand: Our earthly life is difficult and often painful. Our disasters are severe and so, then, is our craving for stimulation, entertainment, distraction, soothing, and even numbing, sometimes to the point of compelling some damaging choices. A curiosity about the darker energies around and within us is a natural human tendency. But while understanding and embracing our own shadowy qualities can aid inner balance, a consuming focus on negative forces against which we must build boundaries (one of my least favorite topics common in pop spirituality content online) does just that: it consumes the spirit, mind, and body, scrambling or muting their most beneficial powers.

I'd like you to recognize above all else the many expressions of divine energy in and around you as your natural baseline perspective, so my approach is straightforward and practical instead of adding to the dark mystery around mediumship. There's plenty of room for mysticism with an uncanny, otherworldly style as long as it's not destructive or misleading, and I can appreciate that we sometimes need the most soul-stirring encounters to startle us into a new perspective. I don't intend to take away the mystique of connecting through our natural mystic gifts. It is magical, even sometimes a little spooky, and always palpably energizing to make a direct connection with spirit. So please dive into this chapter ready for awe and delight at the discoveries you'll make.

At this stage of the book, you're keenly aware of your nature as a spirit being with physical and mental mechanisms that engage you fully in human experience. In the workings of the unique apparatus that you are as a human, your beliefs about divine and earthly influences on your path have a strong effect on how you connect to spirit. As you continue the practice you've set in motion to notice your thoughts and sensations as you take in the abundant signs of spirit around you every day, this chapter focuses entirely on your ability to call on individual and collective spirit entities with focused intention for even more powerful effect in your life (and the lives of others).

Preparing with Faith, Asking with Purpose

The two elements of intentional mediumship that matter the most in my experience are the preparation of yourself as the receptor for spirit connection and the nuanced skill of asking. Rather than prescribing a list of must-do steps for your preparation, I'm going to explain the purpose of the steps that I take to make a reliable connection with spirit for my clients or my own guidance. Through trial and error, observation of other practices I've seen over the years of developing mediumship with others, and a whole lot of marvelous spirit sessions with clients, I've created a short list we'll call "conditions" rather than steps. Take your time to experiment with each of these and freely discover your most effective ways to create the conditions in and around your energy that will bridge the opening between you and the spirit presence available to you. The elements you incorporate into your preparation become what I call your "rough draft process." Some days it might feel like work, but ultimately your rough draft process can be a map for the best self-care you've ever done. Even better, there is always room for it to evolve into a more fine-tuned set of actions suited to your unique gifts.

The conducive conditions:

1. YOUR REASON FOR CONNECTING. It is powerfully formative to everything that will happen next to establish a basic and essential agreement between you, your higher self, and the universe of energy around you about your driving reason for connecting with spirit. As I will emphasize more later, when we get into what the world needs from each of us in this era, your power of spirit connection most naturally bends toward a greater divine purpose. You don't need to fully understand the specifics of that purpose to acknowledge that flowing with it will empower you further

than lesser motives can. It's a choice to swim with the current of a stream rather than against it.

Here is an example of a statement you can make, whether memorizing it through repetition in your mind or writing it boldly in your journal: *The guidance I seek from spirit is of divine nature and for the highest purpose of my soul and the souls of others I encounter.*

This principle of purpose favors positive energy and life-affirming wisdom, and it matters to know your purpose when you're connecting with spirit. It's also important for you to know as you connect with other "spiritual people" on your path that having strong psychic gifts is not an automatic indicator of divine insight or even good intentions. As I explained about the draw of the drama, a person with very keen sensitivity can also resonate with energy of much lower vibration and darker nature than is useful to you. That form of energy is not from a divine source, but from an accumulation of negativity born out of the human experience. Affirming you have a higher purpose aligned with the divine is a simple and valuable tool you'll come to appreciate for its concrete effects in your life, as we'll uncover.

Once you've set that intention in a way that feels true and right for you (down to the word choice, length, and tone), take time to explore your alignment with these next conditions.

2. A CLEAR AND "HUMMING" BODY. My experience with spirit readings has shown me that a certain bodily state of readiness invites the richest, most empowering connection. There's a bit of "you'll know it when you feel it" to this condition, but I've come to think of it as a silent humming. When I was a little girl, my sister and I watched a lot of *Sesame Street* and *Mister Rogers' Neighborhood* on TV, and I loved any of their segments showing machinery steadily doing its job. Footage of a bubble

gum factory, animation of a marble running its complex Rube Goldberg course, Mr. Rogers describing the up-close workings under a grand piano's hood, all delighted me. I still find it so satisfying to watch complex parts of a whole work in coordinated timing. Visualizing the perfection of complex processes within my own anatomy became a regular way I coped with the effects of lupus when it stormed through me painfully. All of this is to say that the first conditions I devote my attention to caring for in preparation for connecting with spirit are physical, as I described in this book's first chapter.

Upright posture, relaxed muscles, steady and comfortable breathing, a lightly satisfied stomach, peaceful surroundings (the immediates of loose clothing and minimal jewelry, plus the larger setting of a serene, uplifting space) are basics to help support your connection to spirit in the moment. For longer-term preparation, regular physical exercise is one of the best spiritual tools I can recommend because of the balanced alignment and flow of energy I've found it stimulates. Many people have experienced and written on the spiritual opening they find this way, as a quick online search of "spirituality and running" reminds me when I need inspiration. The most diligently practicing yogis or my friend Antonio and his blend of martial arts that I shared in Chapter 1 also show ways to an enlightened state through intentional movement.

What we eat and drink has a strong energetic effect too, naturally. Vegans proclaim they notice powerful changes in their spiritual sense of wellness thanks to a diet more directly sourced from nature. I drink certain herbal teas every day, and especially right before meeting a client for a spirit session. Whatever your preferences are from among the bountiful anecdotal and scientific advice out there, I think you'll find that you can identify a clear relationship between your body's state of well-being and your spiritual effectiveness. What helps you tune in to that silent humming throughout your miraculous systems?

3. EQUANIMITY. Emotions and thoughts have their own significant energetic power, as we explored in Part I. When we prepare to connect intentionally with spirit for direct and detailed guidance, it's important that we clear our energy of extreme emotions and engage any activity that helps promote a calm and open state. Spirit presence holds a range of energetic vibrations just as we do, and we aim to meet the most helpful messages in their mood, so to speak. The baseline mental-emotional condition I aim for as I prepare to connect with spirit could best be called "well pleased." This not-too-exuberant but joyful place keeps me open to a wide range of details from the spirit world and helps me avoid feeling attached to a specific outcome in a reading.

Finding the right emotional conditions takes plenty of experimenting, just as cultivating your body's clear and ready state does. To vibrate high enough for a spirit connection, you can start with a feeling of powerful reverence. If we can reach a high-flying state (naturally, not by ingesting substances), it's easy to settle down a bit from there into the light sense of ease and well-being (equanimity) that welcomes in the many kinds of spirit guidance that provide helpful, detailed insight.

4. AGILE RECEPTIVITY. The first three conditions support your eventual ability to adjust to, blend with, and even specifically aim for the spirit connections you make through agile receptivity. We will not receive details from an energetic being unless we vibrate in sync with it first. Every aspect of your preparation of your state of being will determine your energetic range for meeting up with spirit presence. In other words, as I've explained it to workshop students, you aren't going to connect with guidance from the lofty, unconditionally loving angelic realm when your

stomach is in knots and your mind is reeling from a family argument over greasy pastrami burgers. You must resonate with the energy you want to receive.

The condition of agile receptivity takes the most nuanced and sophisticated body-mind-spirit self-knowledge and puts it to very good use, so as you progress through your life's most challenging personal experiences, have faith that they are providing you with opportunity to gain awareness that serves your connection to spirit. The even better news is that extensive personal suffering isn't a prerequisite for highly intuitive mediumship. The school of hard knocks can be a marvelous training ground for body-mind-spirit agility, but there are other ways to grow that skill too.

You can learn to recognize and make shifts to your energy and develop a set of personal energy magic tricks as you experiment with your rough draft process for connecting with spirit. Maybe you've noticed a certain band's music always sends your heart soaring, no matter how terrible you felt before listening to it. Maybe you've noticed that a specific teacher at your yoga studio feels like family to you, and being in her class for an hour cultivates physical well-being plus the sense of familial affection that lets you resonate with ancestors in spirit. Or maybe what warms your soul is the scent of a favorite food, a photo from your most poignant moment, or a visit to the woods behind your parents' house. Whatever it is, find what provokes your magic and use it to adjust the quality of your energetic state.

The Quality of "The Ask"

What's next? You have a principle of purpose for why you're making direct connection with spirit. You've put plenty of time and energy into the preparation of your body-mind-spirit conditions. And now you're ready for the payoff: that high-flying experience of receiving a spirit presence through discernible, specific communication. All that's left is to learn how to ask with your energy so that divine grace steps in and makes the rest easy.

If you want to start with a literal spoken request (tapping in to that power of repeated sacred language and ritual we explored earlier), you can use your purpose principle as an opening and welcome spirit to share information that will be most supportive to you and anyone you're helping. To use a spoken request, be clear about why you are reaching out to spirit; something like "The guidance I seek from spirit is of divine nature and for the highest purpose of my soul" will clarify that your intention is purehearted. Otherwise, your job is to ask energetically, letting your spiritual gifts (i.e., those "clair" senses we talked about in Chapter 4) take over your whole being. They'll activate as soon as you shift your focus from your material surroundings to the spirit energy around you. Whether meditating for a few minutes, listening to a certain song, or staring into a candle flame does the trick for you, use your favorite cue to make that short trip with your attention. Then have faith your natural gifts will help you listen, feel, see, and know whose spirit is present, without pushing or reaching.

If you're like my workshop students—or most anyone I tell about my work for the first time—your next question is "How do you know if it's working?" What you receive through clair senses may be subtle to the point that you can't believe you should give it any credence. That's actually a great sign your connection to spirit is working! It's your role to let that light, light energy gain some ground in you as the human vessel in this connection. You can trust those faint details enough to speak them out loud, write them down, or otherwise acknowledge their guidance. As soon as you do, you'll notice their energy grow a little clearer, bolder, and more detailed. You are the spiritual bellows fanning the flame of the message with your attention to it. There's (literally) no skin off the spirit's back if you miss what they're offering, and there will always be more messages where those missed details came from if you keep an open attitude and continue trying.

TRY THIS: The very best way to strengthen your pathway to spiritual guidance is to try a spirit reading with others and see just how powerful and accurate your senses are for details only they can confirm. All of the previous "try this" exercises in this book are preparation enough for you to jump in and give it a go with a willing participant. As often as and in whatever variety of situations you're comfortable with, ask people around you if they'd be willing to help you as the "sitter" for a reading. That role calls for their openness as well: both to your intercession in asking for spirit guidance connected to them and their life, and to your desire for specific feedback about anything that feels to them like an accurate "hit," resonating with their experience, or feels off and doesn't fit anything or anyone they recognize. The best practice sitters are people you don't already know well. They (and you!) will be most moved by the details you would have no other way to know about them and their important people in spirit.

Keep in mind that you won't translate every sign and message in precisely the way your listener will feel its meaning fits them. You also might have it right, while they aren't in sync to absorb the details. I cannot count the number of times that clients have reached out well after a spirit reading to tell me they've realized I was on point about something they'd denied during the session: "Guess what! I just remembered I *did* have an old friend who died suddenly in their twenties," or, "Yes, it turns out my mom *did* have a miscarriage the year before I was born!"

As you practice your connection to spirit, keep speaking about what you're seeing, feeling, or otherwise noticing, even if it feels silly or a little unbelievable to you. We can only learn from our misinterpretations if we keep the flow of the exchange going. The more you open yourself to understanding and learning from those misses and keep practicing a more nuanced translation of what you receive, the more accurate you'll consistently be in reading spirit.

Avoiding Negative Energy and False Messages

One of our most important responsibilities to ourselves and others in connecting with spirit is to keep hold of the reins of our own energetic vibration, even through life's negative encounters. That equanimity we strive for is not the same as a constant bliss, a deliberate ignorance of the world's woes, or the ability to uphold perfect morals. Instead, it's about choosing our focus and learning to calibrate our body-mind-spirit apparatus toward divine nature in a variety of circumstances.

As I mentioned earlier, a person can have strong sensitivity to energy but not have the knowledge (or even the intention) to steer past a false interpretation of what they're sensing. The gift of spirit sensitivity is naturally endowed, and like any gift it can be wasted or wielded poorly, but in the best cases it is used wisely. Continually honing our spiritual abilities through focused awareness and practice helps us move through bad experiences that might otherwise be debilitating. An essential part of your journey with spirit is to learn how to establish your spiritual grounding in the divine so that you are resilient in the face of distracting or harmful energy.

In some of your life's different stages (which we'll get to examine in detail in Chapter 10), you may have noticed that your brightly activated spirit has been like a flame that draws a wide range of moths. Whether in the form of unwanted attention, toxic personality types, or even exciting events that seem positive but end up overwhelming you, these experiences have something in common: they are different expressions of intense energy attracted to your powerful energy as an actively transforming soul. It can feel, through no fault of your own, like you're spending much of your life regaining your footing after being tossed by a stormy sea of events and people. That pattern doesn't mean toxicity is seeking you out, or that it's your destiny to heal every broken situation you encounter in others, or that life is misery in order to earn a heavenly reward after we die. Instead, it is a signal that your gifts are lighting you up for the world on an energetic level and that you and everyone else will benefit from your intentional work on cultivating them.

Handling Hazards on the Spirituality Trail

Our gifts and the specific lives we lead don't precisely match those of anyone else, so the things we fear, fight, and run from are different for each of us. Even if I were able to capture every form of negative energy into a list of warnings for you, I wouldn't. Itemizing and studying the bad stuff only adds to its power, I've found. Dispelling energy away from it is our goal. That doesn't mean we ignore facts; in dealing with a situation or condition that's causing grief, whether personal or global, I don't encourage blind positivity as a spiritual tool. In fact, I remind clients and students often that a strong connection to spirit only serves you if it is helping you remain grounded in the physical world.

So how do you strike a balance with realism, practicality, and divine perspective all playing a role in the mix?

My Story: The Power of a Glance

If I refer somewhat casually to dark energy or negativity, the dismissiveness comes from hard-earned experience. As I've mentioned about my background, my early years in an idyllic, if somewhat repressed, community were safe and rich with loving extended family, good schools, and reliable traditions. Other than the strange voices I heard that no one around me acknowledged and the strong but invisible sensations I had in reaction to other people's emotional states, my childhood exposure to real-world, material danger was minimal (though I did grow up in Southern California, where the news regularly promised an earthquake called "the big one" would happen any day, and one summer a serial killer dubbed the Night Stalker roamed freely through our neighborhoods). Even though I had plenty of childhood fears, I never really had to confront them.

When I reached young adulthood, however, my spiritual abilities suddenly broke loose like a teenager's raging hormones. The problem with this transformation, which began in silence inside me, was that I was entirely without resources, information, peer support, or tribal elders to tell me what was going on or how to cope with it. I lived in a Los Angeles suburb where moms drove carpool in minivans, kids played soccer and the violin, and dads showed up at six for dinner. When I started having attacks of anxiety and panic that took over my body in crowded restaurants, on hiking trails, or in my own kitchen, I had no guess as to what the source could be other than something very wrong with me or my life choices. When I woke up in the night to being physically dragged across my own bed by something I couldn't see, I thought I must be doing something that deserved a devilish punishment. When my young marriage eventually crumbled under this hidden chaos and I started to attract every wounded soul in the form of toxic, abusive manipulators, I began to guess I might have drawn the short straw and was paying for generations of marital dysfunction before me.

I could not know—not until I followed an instinctive trail that led me to visit a psychic medium on LA's Westside, pull books from a section of the bookstore I'd never noticed, and attend many gatherings with psychic people I'd never have guessed I could relate to—that the dark forces I'd been living with for years weren't some tragic fate or payback for my personal flaws; they were accumulations of energy and I had the ability to counter them. Just not head-on. Fighting made new chaos, not to mention I felt like my body was beginning to melt with the inflammation and infections that my doctors had trouble fixing.

Around this time, I discovered my technique for regaining my balance in the face of something horrible or fearsome. For a long time I thought of it as my "'sup?" glance, as in the "Whassup" a tough kid at school might give you with a quick once-over before moving on as if you don't exist. A more constructive name would be the assess-and-adjust trick. To assess a negative situation or presence, you do have to actually look at it, don't you? But here is the key: you don't have to look for long. When I noticed I could move my gaze firmly toward what I wanted rather than staying focused on what I didn't want, I was amazed by how quickly I could move beyond any negativity that had its grip on me. It worked when I was brand-new to mediumship and heard a voice in a meditation tell me that someone I loved was going to die; it worked in business meetings at my day job when a difficult coworker threatened to take over the energy of a project; and it worked in a lot of horrible moments in between.

Finding the power of that one-two move of an assessing glance plus an immediate adjustment of my own energy to flow with what I now know is the always-reliable, all-inclusive divine energy of the universe changed everything about my life.

Giving your life's hardest challenges just a momentary glance may sound like an impossible prospect in the middle of your own trials. Please understand that I don't mean to deny or make light of anyone's suffering. Once I saw the power of our internal divine spirit to guide us naturally out of that suffering, I knew the energy work of mediumship was a key to something bigger than getting messages from dead people. The more you experiment with your ability to connect directly with spirit, the more you'll realize divine forms of presence never affirm our despair. You'll come to know and treasure the visceral reward of giving negative energy only a short glance, and otherwise returning your attention to the wealth of guidance, reassurance, and strength in the divine nature to which we all belong.

Still Not Feeling It?

I can only assure you for so long that my experience with divine spirit and the incredible moments of connection I've seen in my clients make the process of honing your tools of spiritual discernment worthwhile. Until you feel and know the difference for yourself firsthand, the concept of intentionally inviting "divine" versus "dark" spirit energy sounds like, as my dad would say, a pretty goofball idea. Thankfully, your most powerful natural tools for accessing an experience of the divine don't take a lot of mental or physical muscle.

Here are some of my favorite ways to align naturally with the divine, which you'll recognize from Part I and can try even during the hardest moments in your life:

1. A SHORT BURST OF PHYSICAL EXERCISE.   We know
modern medicine strongly supports regular exercise to stave off all kinds of

illnesses and that spiritual teachers from many traditions also speak to the importance of considering our bodies as "temples" for the divine. A strong and healthy body not only benefits our mental and spiritual states over time, but working the body hard in a short burst helps us overcome acute feelings of negativity. I like to remind anyone who will listen that motion is divine medicine!

2. A BRIGHT DOME OF LIGHT. In those early encounters I had with what many people might call "evil spirits," the overwhelming feeling I had was a sort of enormous doom with an intense sadness or fear. More than once I felt like I was being physically dragged or pressed down flat by an unbearably heavy and threatening energy. Yet, somehow even in the paralysis of my scariest moments, I could still remember tips I'd learned about visualization and try them. Relying on imagination seemed like a weak response to the heavy force I was up against, but every time I was able to conjure the certain conviction that I was surrounded by a dome of divine energetic glow, the threatening energy disintegrated. And not in a slow retreat—it vanished instantly.

3. POWERFUL WORDS, MUSIC, OR OTHER ART. Your soul-centered connection with artists, writers, speakers, and other leaders in creative thought offers a trove of divine power. A client I've connected with in many readings shared that she saw an adversarial relationship become cordial after making sure she always listened to a favorite song before meeting with the other person. Instead of waiting until after the negative energy brought her down, she pre-empowered herself through music. I'm sure you've encountered anecdotes or research that vouch for the positive effect works of art and literature have on our sense of well-being. Believe it, then test it.

4. TACTILE TIME WITH ANIMALS AND NATURE. Whether it's petting a dog, digging a hole in the sand, or walking barefoot on grass, any

simple contact with the natural world brings us gently into alignment with life-giving energy. One of my favorite natural objects to have on hand when I was first learning to prepare to connect with spirit for a client reading was a piece of palo santo; Spanish for "holy wood" and a product of a specific fragrant tree, palo santo is used in Indigenous and mestizo Latin American traditions, by many holistic healers, and in Catholic church ceremonies in Latin America, which I point out in awareness of rampant cultural appropriation of the sacred traditions of oppressed people throughout history.[15] While I honor and promote what I believe is a universal positive human response to nature, I encourage you to investigate the origins of any popular spiritual trends you consider adopting and determine their personal relevance to you. Strongly positive childhood associations I have both with the native chaparral of California and with the scent of cut lumber around my dad's continual projects take me to a higher energy just by looking at the layers of a piece of palo santo and smelling its soothing, earthy fragrance. Standing in the waves of the ocean or running my fingers over stones or shells opens my pathway to the divine too. You'll know your own best tactile choices in nature by those feelings of reverence and peace highlighted in Chapter 3.

Keep using any of these tricks that you notice work well to move your energy from heavy and murky to uplifting and bright. With practice you'll begin to realize that while you're out there in the middle of life's real trials, still mingling with positive and negative moments, you have less fear, anxiety, or anger. Instead, you'll catch glimpses of something wonderful: your quiet, awesome power.

---

15 Martin, Crystal, "Is Palo Santo Endangered?" *The New York Times*, December 16, 2019, https://www.nytimes.com/2019/12/16/style/self-care/palo-santo-wood-endangered.html.

9

Divining Aids: Try New
Tools of Connection

When I first began learning to use my abilities as a spirit medium, my view of divining tools was not very . . . respectful, let's say. I grew up with no more than a passing idea from the movies of what a séance or a crystal ball was, and while a Ouija board might be a fun party game to some people, I couldn't mess around with clichés if I was going to integrate the strange spiritual phenomena I was experiencing into the real world I lived in. In my earliest formal development as a medium—when I was actively taking classes, picking up any books on the subject that sparked my curiosity, and practicing cold readings with strangers whenever possible—I was invited to join groups whose members spoke very seriously about things like what kind of crystal is best for a divining pendulum or how to cleanse the energy of an oracle deck. I usually had trouble keeping a straight face about any of it.

Perhaps because I grew up in an extremely pragmatic family and a sarcastic household, earnestly interacting with an object as a messenger for an otherworldly consciousness seemed ridiculous—as in, worthy of ridicule. But then I found myself earnestly in pursuit of answers about the incredible, bizarre, and force-filled things happening to me, and my instinctive path led me to interact regularly with people who not only cared genuinely about crystals but also other things I'd never heard of, like singing bowls and dousing rods. I learned to take on a tone of mild curiosity when discussing this spiritual paraphernalia, and for a long while I relied on the explanation that I'm just a medium who uses my own self as a tool instead of such objects (which was and still is true, even as I came to understand and appreciate divining tools very differently).

Part of my initial dismissal was that background I mentioned, and part was the acquired personality trait of taking things seriously only when they've proven themselves useful to me. As a kid I especially watched and emulated my father, who was a king of the kind of snide, back-row commentary some of us tall kids develop to entertain ourselves and each other while feeling left out of the main action; he also had a very analytical brain and tended to call anything goofy if he found it extraneous, unnecessary, or illogical. For me, the exposure to psychic circles who took a heart-centered, wide-eyed approach to experimenting with spirit communication was transformative. At first a lot of it looked to my analytical eye like earnest embrace of goofiness, but eventually I took on a "When in Rome" mindset and began to jump in and try things without judgment. That's when my spirit-connection learning curve started to flatten and I zoomed ahead in both confidence and ability.

I hope you're starting to see some of those happy results appear through your lighthearted experimentation with spirit too.

Your Apparatus Is Always Your Best Tool

Once I'd been a practicing mystic for many years and had created the clear process I now rely on (and which you'll develop for yourself beginning with your rough draft process from the last chapter), I realized what I'd had wrong in avoiding divining tools. To me, interacting with spirit presence is as normal a part of my day as thanking a guy who holds the elevator door open or chatting with friends over coffee. I love the reassuring knowledge that there is no "other side" where dead people go, just different forms our energy takes—and I want to help as many people as possible find their own access to that awareness. Where I was misguided was in my assumption that by using a deck of tarot cards or looking into a crystal ball, a person automatically gives away their own superpower, at least in function, to an object. In the best use of them, that's not what's happening with divining tools.

Monica's Story: The Power of Physicality

My friend Monica has an approach to incorporating a whole array of divining tools into her real (and quite "normal") life that sets a beautiful example for every part of life. Her ability to choose to dance with the energy of an object—or with another autonomous person, or with the collective energy of an institution—while maintaining her two feet securely on the ground with unassuming confidence is a practiced skill.

Monica is one of the many people in my world who were once mere acquaintances but became much closer friends after I opened up fully with my own spiritual abilities (another perk of this balancing you're doing of your body-mind-spirit self: more deep and genuine friendships!). When she heard through our social connections many years ago that I had started to practice mediumship, Monica approached me at a lunch gathering to say she'd really like to have a spirit reading with me sometime. I didn't know how primed she already was for her own gifts of spirit connection to burst out and joyfully infiltrate every corner of her life. What I'd get to witness, over the course of many individual sessions and a few of my workshops that she joined in the subsequent years, was Monica's gift for gliding. This gliding is a wonderful mix of seeming both grounded and floating at the same time: the way an expert ballroom dancer can move around the floor without her skirt revealing her feet are moving at all—or better, the way a hovercraft travels from place to place neither up in the ether nor attached to the ground.

What does all this have to do with divining tools? I hadn't thought of the connection until Monica and I were catching up on the phone not long ago. She had been traveling the world solo for months, her fantastic idea to renew and refresh her body, mind, and spirit after having gone through tough family situations that she was shouldering entirely on her own. She took off without a firm plan beyond her initial landing spot at our mutual friend's coastal home in Ireland.

"I didn't pack much, but I packed my cards," Monica said about the multiple decks of the tarot and oracle messages she uses regularly. "Especially the ones that I feel are connected to my mom. And I took a bag of crystals and stones my daughter gave me."

Monica's mother died many years ago, leaving her to look after her aging father and a sibling who had dire mental health challenges requiring special care. She also has raised her daughter as a single parent, as I've done with my kids, and we've often compared notes about relying too much on the stoicism passed down through our heritage—hers German, mine Scandinavian—to get through some of life's bring-you-to-your-knees struggles. But I've noticed that even when she faces extreme pressure with quiet toughness, the whole of Monica seems to pour out from a place of soft warmth. She's able to dole out incredibly keen and supportive wisdom to young people she mentors as a career coach, friends going through trials of their own, and her daughter's friends who've needed a safe respite from traumatic moments of young adulthood. I see Monica give and give and give, all the while seeming to glide gracefully, just beyond harm to her spirit. It isn't easy or particularly magical, but it is exactly how divine energy operates.

When Monica told me how often she consulted oracle cards while she was traveling—to help her decide whether to go to a certain city, for confirmation or guidance about her worries over her family's well-being in her absence, and for ways to interpret the many spirit signs she encountered along the way—she shared something I hadn't realized in all the years we've been friends: she always associated one deck of cards in particular with her mom. The artwork and the language of those cards ring true to the soul she knows her mother to be, so it was an instant and automatic association. Heeding what they say to her when she draws one or a handful for guidance, on the other hand, is an intentional choice as Monica explains it.

"With my mom's deck I would say that's my conduit to talk with her," she told me. "And every time it's so right on, like a connection in its purest form."

When I asked Monica how she'd describe for other people the feeling that lets her know, instead of hope or belief, that the messages that show up in her card readings are meant for her and coming from her mother's soul, she had one of the most poetically simple but apt descriptions I've heard of the space where we recognize we're genuinely connecting with spirit: "The atmosphere—it's almost translucent, like nothing is separating us anymore."

I could see suddenly that rather than acting as a crutch for someone who hasn't done the "work" of learning to use and trust their own inner spiritual senses, a divining tool is simply an extension of the user's abilities. (I felt pretty silly, actually, when I also realized I would never call a kitchen knife a "crutch" for someone who's using it to chop herbs instead of tearing the leaves by hand; the choice of the tool is a decision to refine the action in a very specific way.) As Monica pointed out, a tool is a clear expression of your personal choice, and so is the way you use it. Divining tools can serve you at whatever level of intensity you'd like—light fun, like testing your intuition, or more powerful stuff, like talking with your dead friends and relatives.

For a very different but related reason, Monica felt a certain reliance on the small bag of crystals from her daughter that she'd taken on her world travels. As she told me, "I hadn't thought about the crystals as being protection until just now when I'm talking about it. They were a heavy bag of rocks, each with its own meaning—and they grounded and connected me to Anja wherever I went because she gave them to me." It's long been part of their mother-daughter spiritual culture to give each other small items when they travel; for example, one will lend the other a ring or slip a charm into the other's luggage. The meaning in this practice comes through the energetic details of those objects, which, as we've already discussed, is a form of spirit energy. Using an inanimate object, whether for protection or guidance, is an energetic interaction.

"Their power comes through trusting yourself, essentially," Monica pointed out. "Being comfortable in the knowledge that this conduit is going to be the pathway you take and relying on it for what you've asked it to show you."

An Endless Menu of Choices

I'll remind you as often as you need to hear it: Your body-mind-spirit apparatus is enough for you to connect with spirit and translate details from its energy. You're like the wild horse who knows before a storm appears that it's time to lead his family to high ground under a sturdy live oak. You have the extrasensory gifts built in for what you need to know.

And simultaneously, humans are very inventive about making and using tools. Tools can be marvelous aids for efficiency and a means to go further or deeper into an endeavor than we'd otherwise go. Using our built-in intuitive gifts, divining tools help bring spirit into the physical, as oracle cards have done for Monica, deepening her relationship with her mother and other guides in spirit.

For me to appreciate divining tools, I had to grow and experience a lot more life after the Ouija-board silliness of sixth-grade sleepovers (yes, Ouija made the rotation when we weren't playing "Light as a feather, stiff as a board" or chanting "Bloody Mary" in a dark bathroom). When I became an adult, sometime during the stage after I'd participated in enough psychic medium development groups to be confident in my ability to give readings on my own, the YouTube algorithm opened a gate for me to gain more appreciation for divining tools than I'd thought I needed. I had been listening to videos from spiritual thinkers and TED Talks on concepts of energy, so the app guessed I might want to watch some online tarot readers too. Without ever mentioning I'd taken to learning from them, friends and clients started gifting me with the most beautiful variety of cards, talismans, and books that would teach me even more.

TRY THIS: Knowing firsthand that you won't find divining tools useful unless you have your own personal connection with them, here is a non-comprehensive list to get your exploration started. An abundance of information is available online to help you learn whether the origins and history of a particular tool align with your intentions, which is a valuable place to start. For whatever it may light up for you in making your choice, here's what I know about the following spiritual tools and how to make the most of them.

TAROT. Used first for centuries in games, the cards we know as a tarot deck are an apt tool for cartomancy (divination through cards) because their individual characters depict archetypes and their four suits match different aspects of our human nature. The lifelong spiritual journey—or adventure, as I prefer to call it—can be beautifully mapped out in the progression of Major Arcana, particular named or numbered cards in a tarot deck (such as The Fool, The Hermit, The Lovers, etc.), and the details of life between major milestones are represented by the progression of Minor Arcana cards, numbered and royal court cards that correspond to our familiar deck of playing cards (such as two of cups, the equivalent of a two of hearts).

If you're drawn to literary conceptions of the human experience and the artistic representation of ideas, the tarot offers a rich and fun exploration of your intuitive abilities to understand your own path and the paths of others. Watching other tarot card readers studying up on the various meanings people have assigned to each card (often provided in a guidebook with the card decks one purchases) and ultimately coming up with your own structure for interpretation is a rewarding exercise of your spiritual muscles. You may have fun interpreting messages through a deck of what we now consider regular playing cards as well.

ORACLE CARDS. An endless array of oracle decks has burst from the trend of individualized spirituality, and it would be impossible to categorize them all in one way. Browsing through the spiritual section of a bookstore or online is enough to lead you to an oracle collection you'll enjoy sampling for inspiration and guidance. Again, a guidebook will come with the cards to get you started, but developing your own system for using them is the goal.

As Monica's story suggested, creating an atmosphere of connection with spirit while you draw cards can be as simple as the internal choice to attribute the messages you receive to a specific person each time. Your own energy will interact with the cards as you shuffle, spread them out, arrange them in patterns, and otherwise engage them to be your physical representative for the spirit presence you'd like to hear from. Trust and dive in.

CRYSTALS. Anyone drawn most to elements of nature in their spiritual practice might enjoy collecting and working with crystals. Whether you choose to use crystals as a tool for energetic influence around your home or body (for spiritual protection, balancing, empowerment, pacification, etc.) or as divining tools, they are as reassuring a presence as nature itself is but much more portable.

As a little girl I picked up "special rocks" whenever I was outside, including shells of all sorts at the beach (plus what I eventually learned to be sea glass instead of magic sea stones) and arranged them on shelves or hid them in embroidered handkerchiefs from my Nana. It wasn't until I'd been around psychic development classes and later my community of Reiki healers that I understood my childhood habit as an intuitive energetic practice. In this exploration I'd suggest you go into it without words from a book or advice from another person guiding you. You can always go back later and learn what others have to say about your instinctive choices.

PENDULUM. Here is another tool that I'll admit I prejudged from a distance before unwittingly ending up in a circumstance that gave me a chance to get to know it quite differently up close. One of the simplest little tools for divining answers to questions or making decisions between different options, a pendulum requires only your steady hand (or a fixed structure to hang it from if you don't rely on yourself for that) and the intention you bring to your questions. You can buy or make a chart with simple to more complex answers and watch where the pendulum gravitates, or you can "charge" it with your own agreement about which direction of the pendulum's simple rotation will mean a yes or no to you before using it.

In the practice of Reiki healing, I learned to use a pendulum to help me read the relative balance or imbalance of the client's different energy centers: the chakras of their body. After applications of Reiki energy toward each chakra, the pendulum provides a quick check of whether a new balanced flow has been achieved at an energy center. While the Reiki tradition requires specific attunement, training, and practice, this example shows how widely practical a pendulum can be in any situation where you're seeking a specific indication or answer to proceed.

CANDLES AND CANDLE WAX. One of my early meditation teachers offered the suggestion that gazing into a candle flame could help quiet the mental chatter that can keep us from elevating to higher levels where we meet up with the spirit energy that guides us best. I've used that idea in my rough draft preparation process at times, and it's a tip I still pass along to my workshop students. The varying colors and movements of a candle flame also offer a whole array of signs you could also incorporate into divining messages. Just as the choice of crystals helps you understand your gifts and strengths, the choice to use a flame as messenger highlights the kind of energy you best resonate with.

Only recently have I also seen someone use candle wax dripping as a means to read patterns for messages—a sort of Rorschach test of intuitive responses to the shapes you see. Along these same lines, you can look into the configurations of tea leaves remaining at the bottom of a cup, paint spatters on a canvas, and any other creative idea you can come up with to divine meaning from seemingly random patterns. What makes them conduits for spirit messages is your decision and expectation to engage with that tool as your medium for communication. Test out a few materials and find out how distinctly you experience the messages through each one.

TABLE OR OTHER FURNITURE. I associate table readings with the old-fashioned mediumship parlors of the late 1800s when spiritualism was a hot movement in the United States and Europe. (Whenever we think our trends are something new, a little sojourn back in history will often find human beings have grappled along similar paths of exploration plenty of times before.) A sort of cross between a divining pendulum and a Ouija board, the goal of table readings is to show energetic responses through the movements of the extremely light touch of participants seated around the table.

Any tool you use in a group reading experience is going to show the effects of the collective energy of all who are gathered, so the chances for a jumbled or blocked communication are high. As I think back to my gaggle of friends at a sleepover successfully accomplishing a "Light as a feather, stiff as a board" lift nearly to the ceiling, it was clearly a demonstration of our energetic unity as group. It is rarer in adulthood (though entirely possible) to gather a group of people who resonate together so naturally in spite of a wide range of backgrounds. Whatever the outcome, there's always a chance to learn about yourself and the way spirit energy works by experimenting with these tools.

I CHING / BONE CASTING / RUNES / DICE. This category includes any of a number of ancient divination traditions from cultures around the world using a set of tossed objects, and it reminds us that the human practice of using tools to consult with energetic forces has been an instinct since long before you and I became curious about them. The I Ching is actually an ancient Chinese divination text (also known as The Book of Changes) that offers a complex system of interpretations associated with number sets formed with the arrangement of yarrow stalks. Experts more informed than I am wouldn't necessarily group it with the other tools here, but together they show what a wide range of systems for decision-making, guidance, and course correction have been made by spiritual cultures throughout the ages.

PEN AND PAPER (OR COMPUTER KEYBOARD).   I highly recommend automatic writing or unedited stream-of-consciousness typing as a fun and effective way to bring your connection with spirit into physical form. In fact, I find it's something I recommend to people outside the context of spirit connection as well, without calling it a spiritual tool. If you're still just dipping a toe in the waters here, this tool is one of the forms of spirit channeling you can do almost anywhere, at any time, and without calling attention to yourself. The preparation of your body, mind, and spirit here is just as important as it is with any connection, with or without tools, but once you pick up the pen (or start typing), you can enjoy the familiar and grounded sensations of writing while trusting your spiritual senses to engage with the physical act of jotting down whatever you receive. Try it without looking or focusing directly on the paper or screen to enhance the experience of setting aside your egoic mind in the process and letting spirit have its say.

CRYSTAL BALL. I cannot claim any firsthand knowledge about scrying, the practice of looking into something transparent or reflective to deduce information (a mirror or reflective body of water could also work for you). I include this classic symbol of psychic mediumship as an homage, I suppose, to all of the centuries of spurned mystics—most often women—

who've had gifts of awareness to share and teach others. If you have a soft place in your heart for all of the supposed witches burned at the stake, or clairvoyants stoned publicly for the secrets they might reveal, you may also feel drawn to trying out a tool of divination you associate with their historic role. An affinity for pushing against the dominant mainstream power system is not a requirement for developing your natural spiritual gifts, but if you happen to have that instinct, it's worth feeding it and seeing if the act holds meaning for you.

A Word on Ingesting Substances as Spiritual Tools

Despite the obvious differences from the others, I can't leave out of the conversation the use of hallucinogenic substances as a gateway to spiritual insight or overall well-being—not because I recommend it but because it's become such a big part of the cultural conversation about spirituality that I'm approached about it often. Resonant with the hippie era's exploration of altered states of consciousness, today's trend is laced with a lot more hope for solving mental health issues such as anxiety and depression thanks to advances in psychiatry like the use of psilocybin (magic mushrooms) to treat extreme mental disturbance. My work as a mystic does not address nor conflict with the need for that promising medical research. Instead I bring this subject into our exploration of divining tools because the social embrace of hallucinogens including marijuana products, mushrooms, and ayahuasca is getting confused with authentic spiritual progress yet again.

Before I go further, let me make my own natural bias on the topic clear. Growing up as an intensely sensitive empath with an ability to hear and physically feel spirit energy, I had a very hard time being around people under the influence of alcohol or drugs. The accumulated post-traumatic stress I'd overcome from childhood and later intimate relationships was centered in my experience with people in altered states. And it wouldn't have given me PTSD if those loved ones' altered states thanks to alcohol, weed, or mushrooms had called up their divine, life-giving power, would it? There you have the emotional roots of how my opinion has developed about these so-called spiritual tools.

Once I understood that background, even after a lot of time to heal from that trauma, my attunement to essential changes in people's energy did not go away. In fact, it was as I learned to develop that sensitivity for powerful practical use instead of letting it wreak chaos in me that I could identify what was missing from the substance-induced epiphanies so many people have touted. Throughout this book I've described you and me and every being as a body-mind-spirit apparatus. Our greatest power comes through the integration and balance of those components. The aim of activities to build our spiritual awareness—as long as we want to be high-functioning, valuable members of society—is not to detach and release the spirit from its trinity with the body and mind but to bring it into united harmony with them. Every one of the many anecdotal accounts I've listened to as users of a mind-altering substance tried to describe the benefits or new perspective they gained from a chemically induced high has failed to integrate the experience back into grounded day-to-day reality. Missing the cultural immersion where a tribe and shaman support that comprehensive shift or the expert guidance for reentry such as psychiatrists try to offer sufferers of trauma in psilocybin research, the crucial integrity of body-mind-spirit can be lost.

That gap points again to the potential cultural appropriation problem in spirituality trends as I've mentioned. A proliferation of spiritual tourism for people with the privilege to travel brings bits and pieces of other cultures' spiritual practices into the broader population through social media. It's quite possible for an individual with a computer or smartphone to begin equating a personal spiritual journey with taking a trip (physically or chemically), effectively appropriating another culture's substances, rituals, and other tools for connecting with their divine nature without having lifelong firsthand experience of that culture. Overnight enlightenment with the bonus of Instagrammable backdrops has become associated with an ayahuasca ceremony, for example, which is an ancient spiritual practice of using psychoactive plants that can be traced to traditions as far back as 900 BC in South America.[16] One's spiritual culture, one of the "languages" of spirit I described in Chapter 5, is a highly complex landscape for their spiritual life developed over generations, not over a weekend. The context and collective energy over millennia that led an indigenous shaman in the Amazon basin to use ayahuasca are just not accessible to a CEO from LA who's seeking relief from his anxiety and isolation.

I've made it clear how strongly I advocate taking a leap to explore parts of the world unfamiliar to you, learn beautiful ways of life you've never imagined, and bring home valuable new perspective from cultural immersion. But spiritual travel and trips sparked by a hallucinogen cannot replace your own very specific journey of spirituality that demands your fully grounded awareness of your material context and knowledge base.

---

16 Walubita, Tubanji, "Cultural Context and the Beneficial Applications of Ayahuasca," Lake Forest College, February 21, 2020, https://www.lakeforest.edu/news/cultural-context-and-the-beneficial-applications-of-ayahuasca.

The Power in Choosing

In all of the choices you make on your spiritual journey, the true source of your power is energy itself. Whether you choose to share your exploration with other people or keep it to yourself, trust a divining tool or rely solely on your own apparatus, intentionally spark a new perspective using a hallucinogen or patiently experiment with a natural diet and regular meditation, every one of the selections you make on your path will incorporate your intentions, the energetic heritage you carry, and the preparation you do for your present energy to make the most of an experience. Consider spiritual tools as part of an endless menu you can partake in at your own pace and with your own purpose in mind. The more you try tools that are new to you, the sooner you'll develop an instinct for whether or not a particular tool is meaningful to you.

Part IV

Your Expansive Life as Spirit

Part IV

10

Spiritual Stages: Jump In and Trust the Current

I get really excited about the conversation in this last section of the book (in my mind, this book is a conversation—talking through some of the most complicated, marvelous things about being human, even though you're there and I'm here). It's time to get real, because now we get to take all the pieces of knowledge about our intricate body-mind-spirit abilities and apply them to our everyday, real-life experience for practical use. But one problem with applying the term "real-life experience" here. The whole of our spiritual life that we've been examining so far is as "real" as can be. Your divine nature is an inextricable quality of your real life whether it's acknowledged or not. There's also the issue that we tend to apply negative connotations to what's real. "You need to face reality" doesn't usually mean "Hey, let's take a look at all of the wonder your real life holds!"

Instead, let's bring the expansive sensations of connecting with spirit into our activities, relationships, and daily purpose for living a physical existence. Let's make sure your life itself is as expansive as divine energy.

The Anatomy of a River

A metaphor I use frequently with my clients and students to help them feel spirit's presence is a flowing stream. We might travel alongside a river and rarely acknowledge it's there unless we happen to cross its path, or we can step into it, enjoy its natural current, and discover how to function differently within its flow. Once we've chosen to travel by water, we have a wealth of new choices to make for how we'll use the tools we have for the journey and many new things we'll experience about the natural surroundings we were part of all along. There is always a choice with this river, whether you'll fully jump in (such as a mystic of any tradition might do in devoting their life to the engagement of divine spirit) or you'll just occasionally hop in to see what the stream offers. The aspect that is not optional in this landscape of intertwined water and earth is its anatomy: the headwaters and tributaries, splits in the channel, natural curves and flat deltas, the strength of the roaring current that's overwhelming in places and almost imperceptibly in motion elsewhere.

Your spiritual stages are part of nature's way. Certain conditions in specific order will turn a pupa into a fully grown insect, a seed into a large, beautiful plant. The seasons in a year all hold unique value, and each individual life going through them receives distinct benefits. Our own bodies change with the seasons and their effect on the sky, the temperature, the barometric pressure, and the animals who grow or shed their coats that time of year. Every organism and system on Earth engages in these coordinated life cycles, each with its own purpose. And you are blessedly part of that universe in body, mind, and spirit. To fight against or dismiss the value in any stage of your life's course is both futile and unfortunate; each part of the landscape holds beauty and purpose to relish.

One of my extremely selfish reasons for loving the work I do with clients is that each person I see is in a different stage of their spiritual journey, and with every spirit reading, I recognize processes I've been through or still anticipate for myself. It is a reassurance to me that we're all sharing in something in this great moving force of life that is purposeful and intelligent—maybe even brilliant—that we sometimes call "divine timing." The thing we often forget to appreciate about divine timing is that our divine nature is full of complexity that we in our human perspective could never work out: the perfect logic of an outcome that we couldn't see at the outset, a seemingly miraculous coincidence of events, or the coordinated layers of synchronicities that become our experience. The systems working together in divine brilliance create distinct stages in our lives that we do not control, but the tools we develop to engage our full spiritual abilities with our bodies and minds sure do make the journey along the way better.

You're Both the Hero and the Antagonist

I'll lay out the vital spiritual stages here as I've both witnessed and passed through them, along with points of guidance culled from spirit readings and those "passive encounters" with spirit energy we considered in Part II. What I ask of you from here forward is to shift a little in your seat and begin looking at your own everyday experiences from a new view. Consider them through the divine frame that you were born with and have been reconstructing for yourself through this book's exercises, which sets you as all of the characters in your story: both hero and challenger, aide and foil. While you are indeed one of billions of living humans and therefore could take your pick of any of those billions to frame as your opponent or savior, the divine spiritual journey you're on is yours alone.

The many other souls you engage with every day are important as teachers and mirrors, but as sources of spiritual well-being? Or the culprits to blame for your challenges at each stage? Other people may do a good job of appearing that powerful, but the power resides with you. You always hold the wheel of your energy with the body-mind-spirit tools you're developing, so you hold the power to ease or burden your own travels along the river of your soul's journey.

As hard as it feels at first to keep your gaze steadily pointed through that divine framing, you'll find that it gets easier the more you practice it. Just like any new skill takes time to feel natural, it also eventually becomes so automatic you'll hardly be able to remember doing it any other way. Considering how tough some of the spiritual stages we go through are to endure, it's worth the intentional choice to see yourself in your full power.

While any of these spiritual stages can happen more than once during your life and may startle you by jumping a place in line now and then, here is the natural succession of spiritual awareness as it develops and changes in these phases of your life.

BIRTH IN INNOCENCE. When we first arrive as a physical creature—setting aside religious beliefs that insist on "original sin"—we are fresh and innocent in spirit, mind, and body. Without dwelling on those scientific and philosophical questions about the nature of human conception that will perpetually divide moral and political debates, we can agree that some qualities are generally common among the newly born: curiosity and wonder, susceptibility to outside influence, and vulnerability to the chaotic jumble of experience as we try to learn what we need to know and navigate our initial growth.

Science offers overwhelming evidence that the care we receive in our first five years of life plays a vital and formative role in our physical and mental development, our immune systems, and our access to social and emotional tools. Likely thanks in part to such evidence, health care, education, and other provisions for young children have been improving globally over the last century. But how well nurtured is the spirit of newly born children or for that matter an adult in a stage of rebirth that carries similar vulnerability? In modern industrialized societies, not very well.

How does a soul begin to learn to hold the reins of their own spirit energy in this stage without instruction? From early childhood and more recent rebirth experience, I know the soul moving through this phase to be the most vigilant and sponge-like. We constantly watch to see if our experience supports or slashes our instinctive assumptions, so the responses of people and events around us become key factors in our learning. And great benefits to the spirit's development happen naturally during this challenging stage of being "the new kid," as we vigorously test our spiritual elasticity. Imagination, creativity, and curiosity are default instincts in the newly born, and all of them are invaluable to our ability to connect intimately with spirit presence later on. These qualities are also hugely susceptible to damage by the bigger, stronger, more seasoned influences around us, which brings us to . . .

QUIETING OF SPIRIT/MATERIAL SELF-EXPANSION Under the powerful sway of the material conditions we experience, the soul conspires in a natural period of intense focus on growing the skills and resources we'll need to survive physically. In extreme cases, this stage extends to nearly the whole of one's life. A constant pursuit of earthly rewards in the form of money, goods, and property or in the form of continuous work toward physical or intellectual dominance can take nearly all of one's energy. This focus is often to the detriment of soul-level gifts taking shape, but it never leads to a wasted stage. And to view this from the other direction, we can never become so spiritually enlightened that our material needs are unimportant. (That stage is called being dearly departed, so in talking about your own life among "spiritual" company, don't ever succumb to pressure to deny or minimize your material achievements.)

While the period of quieted spirit senses will be entirely different depending on your gifts and purpose, it is valuable even for someone who ends up pursuing a primarily spiritual path. I know priests who were first cops or academics and Buddhist monks who were accountants and rocket scientists. Longevity in the physical world allows for many years of disconnect from our sense of divine nature. It is often the imbalance of energies that takes shape in us during this stage that triggers a change into subsequent stages. Our discussion of masculine and feminine energy in the next chapter will shed light on the reasons such imbalance grows.

DISILLUSIONMENT. Anyone who has studied the classic story arc popularized by American writer and mythologist Joseph Campbell as the "hero's journey" is familiar with the importance of a call to adventure early in the hero's experience. Some inciting event must spark a desire to leave the security of what the hero character has known for uncharted territory where new fortunes become possible. In the case of a spiritual journey, self-knowledge and divine awareness are the sought-after treasures. While a human life story does not usually fit into the tidy narrative structure of epic novels and blockbuster movies, a stage of disillusionment on some level is universal and is a crucial propeller into the next stages of a spiritual journey. We have to discover at some point that the people, structures, rules, and assumptions we've been relying on are fallible; otherwise, we don't move forward toward autonomy.

The stage of disillusionment can fill us with fear and cynicism, which trigger self-protective habits. For clients I've worked with, the inciting event has been anything from a loved one's fall from grace in the client's eyes to the corruption of an institution with a big role in their life or newly acquired knowledge that destroys their old assumptions. On the spirit level, this stage can feed a disempowering blockage of energy. We may feel justified to rail against something—whether a person, event, or idea—and we cloud the spaces in our bodies and surroundings where divine energy wants to flow freely. Even the most righteous battles can have this effect, as we can witness in the lives of many activists who take up noble social or environmental causes. There is a subtle but powerful energetic difference between fighting against an injustice and promoting the creation of a new solution.

THE CRASH. In every human life, and especially for anyone I know to be on an intensely spiritual path, the experience of a "crash" is inevitable. Any personal loss, shock, or cataclysmic change that brings us to our knees counts as a crash. The event doesn't need to be obviously destructive in the eyes of anyone else for your loss to be significant to you. Whether it's a divorce, a cancer diagnosis, the loss of a job or home you love, or simply a sudden internal recognition of your essential solitude in the world, the experience qualifies as a crash because it sends you into what Spanish mystic John of the Cross termed the "dark night of the soul." In that place of disconnect from hope or direction, you might feel ennui or more intense suffering. But within that abyss, like in the darkness of rich soil, germination is possible.

I once heard a tarot card reader refer to the crash as the "earning your grit" stage and instantly recognized what she meant because of how crucial my own dark nights were to my eventually growing the thick skin that better protects a soft heart. I'd clarify the idea to say that the crash is just the beginning; it's the side effects and aftermath of a crash that teach and test us, requiring us to let go of habits, relationships, and thought patterns that cannot serve us on our paths any further and to find the will to reset and move forward.

REBIRTH AND AWAKENING. Sometime during the period when we wallow or flail around in a dark abyss after the crash, our whole body-mind-spirit apparatus goes through a softening we can call surrender. On an energetic level, it means we become more porous again, like the wide-open-with-wonder newborn who welcomes knowledge and life. Only this time, the earned wisdom of past experience helps shape our next steps.

The spiritual awakening that takes place during this stage has its own many subparts and phases, which mystics, yogis, some clerics, and unanointed but wise accidental teachers might explain by saying that you are returning to your true self. In my work with students and clients, my approach to moving through spiritual awakening is tool-based so that you can find the language that most means "awake" to you. Many phrases for awakening in modern pop spirituality—"the truth behind the veil," "as above, so below," "get into the vortex," and "oneness with the universe," to name a few—have been borrowed from other teachers and traditions and repeated so extensively that eventually the problems with institutionalized religion, like disconnect from meaning and apathy toward divine purpose, could easily resurface again. I'd rather you awaken to the natural tools you have of body, mind, and spirit and discover for yourself what they are there to show you.

LIVING WITH PURPOSE. When you have been experimenting with your own spiritual power for long enough to feel it is an integrated part of your nature, you begin to be empowered to do the work the universe really needs from you. It's natural to conflate this stage with discovering your ideal career or finding the home and community of your destiny. As annoying as it is, I have to add the "life is a journey, not a destination" reminder to keep you light on your feet when it comes to the idea of purpose. There is dynamic motion in living; it's not a static landing pad.

With that somewhat irritating but liberating truth understood, we'll look in-depth at what living with purpose is a bit later, but for now you can count on it having something to do with those unique spirit senses you've been learning to use thus far.

TEACHING OTHERS. We become teachers for others at every spiritual stage, whether we mean to or not. As any parent knows, however, it feels better to be the kind who teaches from positivity, sharing wisdom and expertise to guide children toward better outcomes rather than from negativity focused around what not to do without explanation. After a cycle of significant challenge, softening, and new birth (of perspective, skill, or integration of the two), we are particularly primed to impart what we've learned along the way for others who are in a place of struggle.

Perhaps the most important spiritual ability you'll tap in to during your stage as a teacher is your trust in life and the universe to provide what each of us needs to learn naturally. With that faith secured in you, you'll offer your ability to guide, comfort, assure, and enlighten others as an instrument of the divine, using your wisdom as needed for another soul's expansion. If instead you get caught up in impressing your specific expectations on someone you're in a position to teach, those tools you've honed become less effective. An energy of detached wisdom is essential for a teaching stage to be effective. Perhaps the oldest living people are able to achieve that state with the most grace because they have lived through enough versions of a spiritual life cycle to be entirely surrendered to its natural outcome. If you and I are lucky enough to find out for ourselves by reaching that state, we can certainly consider our lives well lived.

TRY THIS: It's time to celebrate your own spiritual stages for all they offer and show you about yourself and the greater universe through a work of art. The best ways I know to honor your soul's journey all call for some form of creative expression—the symbolic, artistic, visionary ways we humans capture and convey what matters most to us. In the process of creating something original, we always, always, always uncover even more truth than we knew we'd be expressing when we started. So please do this for yourself and trust both the process and the result to be worth your time and any effort it takes to set yourself free to create.

A few starting-point suggestions: Give yourself a ten- to fifteen-minute window of quiet to meditate, ponder, or daydream about how you've experienced the stages I've described. For any spiritual stage you have yet to experience, you can call on your visionary gifts and express what they show you. Maybe your spiritual stages look like a system you can draw, diagram, or paint; if that's the case, get yourself a big piece of paper or canvas to play on until you've depicted the journey you recognize. Your stages might each evoke songs you love and inspire you to create a playlist all about and for yourself. Or maybe the phases of spiritual growth, quieting, expansion, death, and rebirth you've experienced express themselves as individual creations of totally different formats because they stand in such extreme contrast to each other.

I also need to say here that I know making art is not something everyone feels comfortable, knowledgeable, or well supplied enough to do. If you're like the many people who haven't been encouraged or taught to express themselves creatively through art, I understand that you may be hesitant to do this exercise. If so, the gentle reminders I want to offer you are that (1) since the days of cave paintings, humans have had an instinct to depict life through art, so it is also in you to be artistic, as rudimentary as your tools or training may be; (2) scientists have found that other animal species engage in art-making, and so if an elephant can be creative, you can too; and that (3) this activity won't be graded.[17]

Jamie's Story: The Power of Trust

One of my longtime clients who has come periodically for spirit sessions over many years and stages has shown me so vividly what choosing to flow with the stream of divine energy looks like over time. Jamie reached out years ago after a word-of-mouth connection led her my way for her first spirit reading. I was struck by her peaceful manner, though it belied the thrumming energy I picked up from her soul right away. Jamie was a married mother of one daughter, very focused on the material needs of her husband and child, and was approaching middle age with a disquieted heart and mind. In our earliest session together, a dancing, singing family of spirit presences came forward like a band of guardians around Jamie, with her maternal grandmother leading the charge in song.

Jamie wasn't sure about the heavenly choir I could see and hear, but she humbly admitted, "I have loved to dance my whole life. I don't do it as much anymore since I had my daughter. I've gained weight and just lost touch with it, but I did become a yoga instructor." As the session progressed, each supportive message from spirit for Jamie expressed that she had incredible inner strength and instinct for taking care of anyone she came in contact with—most deeply caring for her family, whose African American heritage, they pointed out, held generations of suffering with unsurpassed strength. She had inherited stoicism I recognized, but with a

---

17 Goldman, Jason G., "Creativity: The weird and wonderful art of animals," BBC.com, July 23, 2014, https://www.bbc.com/future/article/20140723-are-we-the-only-creative-species.

more simmering quality born from a very different kind of necessity than my ancestors or I could know.

In the years that followed, Jamie returned every six months or so for a spirit reading, and I encouraged her to participate in one of my workshops for people to unlock their own gifts for connecting directly with spirit. A group dynamic offers many more opportunities for our energy to light up in response and engagement with others' energy, and I witnessed how gracefully Jamie's spirit interacted with that of every other person in the class. Whether you are a dancer or just a fan who's watched and learned to appreciate dance as an art form, you can understand what I mean in saying she moved like a dancer, even while seated in a chair. The composure and posture, ability to pause without rushing a response, and perfectly synced participation of even her facial muscles in conveying energy were remarkable. During a class session when we worked with nature spirit guides and I saw with each of the other participants an animal that came forward as their symbolic representative and energy protector, Jamie's spirit guide was a waterfall.

The stage Jamie was living through when she first came to see me was the tail end of a long period when she let the material world around her guide her decisions. As time passed while her daughter grew older and her husband's career led them to make a huge move to a different country, Jamie gracefully moved through the changes with her own thrumming energy held down, making space for her dance partners to shine. Our spirit readings revealed how much her body longed to move again in different ways. We talked about the signs she was seeing that she had something to learn from new kinds of relationships, both through social interaction and through mentoring younger people at work. The energy grew around her desire for own abilities to take the wheel instead of the back seat. And water kept showing up in her visions and our spirit readings together—the ocean, a placid stream, another waterfall, this one gentler than the first. Her inner spirit was speaking its language.

However, when the whole world faced a global pandemic that shook our lives, the solid floor under Jamie's life began to crumble. After she left the home where she and her husband had raised their daughter and made the adjustment to living in a new country together, her marriage ended. The complicated decisions Jamie and her husband had to make to divide up their lives included selling the house back home that they'd left in her parents' care, and Jamie found herself without the physical and emotional roots she had long relied on. Before she shared any of these details, the image I remember coming up most prominently in the spirit reading I did with Jamie during that stage was of her letting go of an enormous stack of papers that had been weighing her arms down. In the vision, the paperwork was being strewn in the wind behind her as she rode a bicycle alongside a huge body of water.

For many, many months, Jamie and I didn't connect while she climbed out of her old life and into a new one. When she did reach out for another reading, years after first opening up to the direct connection and guidance from spirit, I told her that I saw an infinity symbol over her aura right before our appointment and it remained there throughout the session. As I channeled the guidance to describe it, I shared: "It is so visible and bright and shining around you, and I feel like it's moving me into an 'infinity dance.' It's telling me the important theme for you right now: you are in a place of reconnecting into the flow, remembering you're part of that infinity symbol, that you have a special way of dancing through life along its curves."

We know this planet and the greater universe that it's part of are shaped by cycles of life, transformation, death, and new birth. As members of that system, we also go through cycles we experience in our own ways. Yet somehow in our very materially oriented existence, we overlook the divine universal mechanisms behind them. As the infinity symbol represents so perfectly, our travels along a soul's spiritual path are varied and interesting. In the dips and curves it takes us through, living as an expression of the universe itself is not a boring circle but a divine pattern that frees us to dance with it. So along with appreciating the nature of your different life stages from a spiritual perspective, your new framing of yourself may just enhance the overall reverence you have for life itself.

And you remember how valuable reverence is for bringing you right up close to divine spirit and sharing its perspective of love, promotion of new life, and ultimate well-being, don't you?

11

The Big Picture: Bring Your Gifts to Everyday Life

Through most of this book I've encouraged you to be self-interested, self-absorbed even, so that you become an expert on your full range of gifts: for navigating your own consciousness, engaging with and framing the outside events that shape the shoreline of your experience, and more intentionally choosing your energetic signature that will attract experiences your way. Such self-study is not selfish but in truth is ultimately a gift to the world, in whose energetic web you dwell. So now at last, let's talk about the way you package and deliver that gift in everyday life, so that it is best put toward addressing the world's needs.

There's another subtle distinction to make here before going further, lest you should think I'm suggesting the whole purpose of getting to know and develop yourself as an integrated body-mind-spirit is to "do good" in the world, serving others. We might automatically draw that line out of religious or moral dogma, but it's not a requirement of your divine spirit, as I hope you're coming to know it instinctively as a guiding presence within you. That benevolence is, however, a natural inclination of divine energy. And here's the reason, I suspect, from the spirit readings that have shown me what our point of view looks like when we've released all earthly fretting: because it is in caring relationships and productive collaboration with others that we expand our natural gifts. Conflict, healing improvement, expansion. Conflict, healing improvement, expansion. It's a pattern of evolution, which we feel divinely guided to participate in, however messy the details of that participation may be.

Interact and Intersperse for Your Own Good

Among the many social creatures on the planet, humans enjoy an especially complex challenge resulting from our inner drive to be in relationships with each other (and with other animals, I want to add as a nature fiend!). We have layers of natural instincts that compete for primacy, though, especially when we're struggling through our most difficult life experiences. The baser forces of our nature may twist us out of touch with our divine spirit's awareness, making the ideal of loving, life-giving cooperation with other people and the emotional agility it requires seem impossible.

The good news in that challenge is the polished gem idea I remind my clients to visualize when life has led them into interactions full of friction. That rubbing up against perspectives, approaches, and goals that seem so contrary to our own is the best way to refine our spiritual gifts, just as a rock is polished into a gem by progressive abrasion using finer and finer grits of harder substance. Whether because a relationship prompts us to a higher awareness or spurs us into a role we might never have guessed we were suited for, I'm convinced the difficulty of interacting with others is as much of a soul-level draw toward them as the companionship we need for thriving. (It's one way I reconcile the irritatingly contradictory concepts of "like attracts like" and "opposites attract.")

So we turn our focus from the fully integrated body-mind-spirit self toward the value of placing that self into the context of group effort. Let the work of considering what the world needs from you—whether in those rock-polishing interpersonal relationships or your societal roles—strengthen your connection to your own divine being.

Bring Your Tools to the Table

Once you feel the positive effects of being in sync with divine energy in your body-mind-spirit, you also catch a glimpse of the notion that all good things are possible from that state of being. As you practice returning to that place of clarity, reverence, and flow, it becomes almost unthinkable that you'd want to approach your everyday life from any other state. How, then, will you bring those floaty, ethereal notions down to the ground for a practical purpose? A good place to start is an investigation of the real-life spiritual tools you uniquely hold.

Beyond all those breathing exercises and nature walks that ready your body as a spirit receptor, the belief inventory that makes you aware of how welcoming your mental landscape is to divine energy, and the reverence you've cultivated to activate your higher being, what are the tools you'll be able to use in the unique life you're leading?

Enlist Your Specific Gifts and Guides

By this point in your practice of sensing, connecting with, and translating spirit presence, you'll likely notice how much your experience of spirit varies as your own body-mind-spirit energy changes, over long periods of the spiritual stages we talked about in the last chapter as well as in little day-to-day variations. An incredible diversity of divine offerings available to and through you will mirror, complement, and support the circumstances and changes you need to dance with in your life.

To find out which spiritual gifts and spirit guides you have to work with, you'll need to keep up your astute observation of your own nature and do your best to let go of preconceived notions or specific outcomes. It may not be easy at first, but that skill develops through joyful, eager experimentation. The kind you've been doing throughout this book!

TRY THIS: Let's help you determine your most natural spiritual gifts. The extrasensory abilities you're most likely to use on your journey and share with the world appear in the patterns of the content you attract from spirit and the ways you receive it. Bring out your journal and jot the thoughts you have in response to these few questions to help you uncover those patterns and their purpose:

- Going back to all of the "clair" senses you learned in Chapter 4, which sense is your keenest at giving you accurate information?
- When do you feel the strongest whoosh of reverence and wonder in your life?
- What kind of information do you notice you're drawing in most often (e.g., emotional content, logistical guidance, historical details and their healing, etc.)?
- To help with some ideas about context, but not to lead you in any of these directions specifically, consider the incredible range of spiritual gifts human beings have, such

as these different abilities I've witnessed in my clients, students, and colleagues in spiritual wellness:

• Clairvoyantly seeing and describing in precise and accurate detail the childhood home of a stranger.

• Feeling a sudden difficulty breathing during a spirit reading until discerning that the listener's father had died from emphysema.

• Holding a small teapot never seen before and being able to thoroughly describe the relationship between the person who gave the pot as a gift and its recipient.

• Hearing from a coworker about his wife's brand-new pregnancy and knowing she would have a set of twins, boy and girl specifically, long before the couple learned that news from their doctor.

• Being given the choice of two blank CD covers and accurately identifying which one holds which music album, countless times in a row with different albums.

• Waking up to see a friend's mother appearing to stand in the bedroom doorway and finding out from that friend later that her mother had just died.

• Meeting people for the first time and accurately knowing how many siblings they have, including gender and birth order.

These abilities of awareness, from the seemingly trivial to the emotionally weighty, are just a small sampling of psychic gifts, mediumship, and powerful intuition at work in people around us every day. My own life and vocation have brought me to witness and learn from these moments continually, ever since I acknowledged there was more to my own human awareness than I'd been taught as a child. The most significant part of these realizations to me is that delving even further into the how and why of a specific spiritual ability always leads to greater clarity about our roles with each other and the world around us. I take it as evidence that our lives are purposeful in different ways.

I encourage you to talk with other people as often as possible about what abilities you've witnessed that may be spiritual gifts. Whether someone you know has an uncanny way of communicating wordlessly with pets or has had prescient dreams without knowing what to do about them, your choice to open up the subject from your heightened state of divine awareness will make your own gifts and theirs more active. After all, how can our full range of spiritual abilities be practical unless we can also speak with each other about them?

Souls Who Guide You

The connection with individual spirit guides or guardians is another widely varying experience that depends on your energetic signature and the needs of your soul's journey. It is significant to know specifically who is present with you in spirit form for many reasons. Just as the content of a living person's words to us carries different meaning depending on who they are to us (the messenger affects our reception as much as the message), we can gain nuanced wisdom from spirit messages when we know some identifying details about their source.

As fellow humans come and go through your life for different amounts of time, the souls in spirit who attend to you can change with your stage and interests. Remember: we are constantly attracting others' energy with our own vibration and focus—though we cannot be consciously aware of every aspect of our own energy, which we inherit through our history and heritage along with shaping it in our present moment. I've sensed many different kinds of spirit presence for clients and students in my work, which tells me how widely varied the roles of spirit guides can be for people, including the following:

- The friend from college they'd always deeply admired.
- An adored pet cat who'd died and brought back wisdom from spirit that felt ancient and vastly observant.
- A childhood teacher they feared but respected.
- A great-grandparent, grandparent, or even distant cousin they'd never even met.
- Nature beings that appeared like fairies or sprites (a concept far outside any tradition I personally hold or had even thought about before, making these guides the most surprising learning experience for me!).
- Souls who were unrelated as human family and seemed to have a higher divine quality composed of a more collective energy. Some practices refer to these guides as different hierarchical levels from "angels" to "ascended masters," but you may have your own terms for what are essentially the same type of presence.

My experience as a medium and spiritual coach tells me any source of energetic guidance, care, and insight can be a spirit guide. As I mentioned in Jamie's story during the last chapter, in many of my workshops I devote a session to tuning in to each participant's spirit animal (which can turn out to be another aspect of nature, as Jamie's "spirit animal" was distinctly a waterfall). These specific beings of nature and the unique qualities they embody always end up being deeply meaningful for the participants in the stage they're in and the particular areas of growth they're undergoing. Most importantly, these guides remind us all that we are essentially made of and united with natural elements ourselves.

Another type of guide I encourage you to invite closer in your practice of connection is a spiritual embodiment of your higher self. Often you'll become aware of its presence because it feels like a family member or soul-bonded friend who knows you with unconditionally loving objectivity. If you're not sure that you've had the blessing of such a relationship in your physical life yet, I'll venture that you have at least imagined one. And I'll take that a step further to tell you that the relationship was not only in your imagination. Just as I can always identify a nature spirit connected with every person I meet, the higher-self spirit guide is part of everyone's existence. It is your most intimate connection to divinity, and whether you meet in meditation or during exercise or while writing in your journal, that particular spirit guide is always patiently ready to connect with you.

Our Collective Unity as Guidance

In this exploration of spirit guides and for your whole journey forward, it will serve you to know that there are times when the swell of emotion in an encounter with spirit and the new sense of knowing it offers something so powerful that it doesn't seem to matter much who specifically is giving it.

In these distinctly high-flying spiritual moments, we are tuned in to broader perspective from the collective wisdom of many ancient souls and feel an immense reassurance that we belong among them.

Ultimately, reaching that level of awareness, even for a moment, is indescribable; it's also unteachable. I believe it belongs to each of us as a birthright, and you'll know it when you experience it. In that state of communing with the divine collective, anything is possible and you are your most creative self. You are also the most at peace without having to accomplish a thing. Just as you are—without consuming, doing, or being anything outside of your own natural state—all divine guidance is yours.

Your Choices Ahead

Any time you've spent to enrich and deepen your relationship with spirit in all its forms, especially getting to know the divine in you and everything you see, cracks open a door. But as you know about opening doors, looking through and stepping through are not the same experience. Essentially, you still have the option at this stage to keep dormant the knowledge and insights you may have gained from the exercises in this book or other spiritual deep dives you've done, staying at that doorway's threshold. Or you can even try to turn back toward the view of the world you had before getting to this doorway, but that likely wouldn't last.

It's next to impossible to unknow what you've discovered, so let's explore how you'd like your daily life to expand with the help of divine energy and the sharing of your unique body-mind-spirit gifts. You've probably noticed in your practice that your awareness of yourself as a powerful apparatus brings up as many new questions as it does answers. The nature of our universe, the roles of different people in our lives, the degree to which we have a purpose to fulfill before we die, all of these topics and so many others become more vibrant when we know our interconnection with spirit.

For many people, that newly cultivated perspective, along with the tools of meditation, breathwork, interpretation of signs, or creative expression of your life path, is more than enough to make this journey worthwhile. I wholeheartedly encourage you to use this experience to achieve whatever level of satisfaction you want from it. If you came to this book with a deep longing to make a bigger leap in a new direction, know that you're empowered to do that too.

Will That Be a Hop, Skip, or Jump?

Let's talk about the size of the leaps that you're going to be taking in this lifetime. Not everyone is living their present physical incarnation for the purpose of stretching the furthest boundaries of social norms or personal security and safety. All of us who live with technology at our fingertips know that these days collective attention turns quickly toward the biggest splash. You don't have to look any further than the TikTok trends that earn people heaps of affirmation (or at least notoriety) by doing the most dangerous or shocking thing on video for public viewing. The new normalcy of such instant fame has given a lot of younger people the idea that their life will not be worth anything unless they're pushing boundaries in a big way.

I want to be very clear that when I talk about taking leaps with your life, I'm including the more subtle, nuanced, personal versions of a leap into the unknown. We do it in the split second of speaking up in a roomful of people where we feel intimidated by the others there and what we think their judgment of us will be. We might take a chance at asking for help, though we've been conditioned to glorify self-sufficiency. Making a choice that's different from what our families have always expected us to do is another one, which I relate to well myself.

Taking a leap out of the reliable box of a marriage I had gotten into from a very young, imbalanced energy—even though it included pulling along my sweet, unwitting children, whom at the time I believed my whole existence was for—meant our little family plunged into less security, less certainty, and less conventional standing in the world than the people who surrounded us had. That leap, while we've ultimately thrived, hurt our hearts in lasting ways. It also led to times when I didn't know how I'd pay for our next groceries, days I went out and sold belongings to pay our utility bill or buy one of the kids a ticket to a dance. We stopped getting invitations to gatherings of the "intact" families and lost contact with friends with whom we couldn't keep up financially. In the fuller landscape I can see from where I sit now, none of those changes were soul-damaging. They were illusion-destroying, grit-earning stages. And they set each of us free to find out what we were made of outside of a box.

Sometimes we're lulled into thinking the most incredible gift, the source of our biggest power, is our free will to choose how far to jump. You do get the choice—on a spiritual level—of what your ratio of comfort to uncertainty will be. Sometimes "comfort" is only comfortable because it's familiar. What we are familiar with and rely on can be some horribly miserable circumstances, and still, we might not be ready to make the choice to take a chance on making a move away from them. What I've noticed, both in my personal life and among the people I've worked with, is that the most truly divine gift is what you might call divine intervention. Whether it looks like good or bad news on the surface, that something that comes along and stirs, jolts, or propels us into making a move despite what our ego might choose is the divine in quiet collaboration with you. The divine has an interest in your changing and growing.

Answering Divine Calls

The first question for most of us would naturally be "How do I know if it's a divine call?" when we feel propelled to move in a new direction with our life. Consider here and now that your comfort with the perpetual new questions this book brings up is also a strong signal of your readiness for your spiritual awareness to change your life. We have an instinctive drive to ask different questions when our souls tell us a bigger shift is imminent. It's not that the spiritual path calls you to a continual state of uncertainty—naturally, you seek out a connection with spirit guidance looking for the opposite. Your relationship with spirit does offer you greater clarity and will continue to do so even more powerfully, as long as you keep asking questions about your life and then let the answers from subtle signs, intuitive interpretations, and the heightened reverence for possibility move you.

Your developing intimate relationship with spirit guidance will also help create the balance you need before taking a leap successfully. (Since I grew up playing basketball, my spiritual shorthand to myself is often, "Square up before you shoot!") Any time you try to take a step off a shaky stance, you find out the results on landing aren't so good, or that it takes a lot more nimbleness in the air to right yourself. Whatever the visual you relate to on a physical level, one of the most important reasons to develop the equanimity we work on for receiving guidance from spirit is that it also readies us for taking chances we might hold back from otherwise. The practice of discovering your best tools for steering clear of negativity turns out to be great help in giving you the balance you need to take marvelous positive leaps in your daily life too.

The Balance of Energies

From the time you took your first breath, you've constantly been channeling opposite, complementary forms of energy that permeate all of nature—feminine and masculine, yin and yang, dark and light, creation and incubation—whether or not you've consciously contemplated their coexistence within you. By intentionally cultivating your ability to view your energetic balances, you will refine the ability to steer through your next life stage and do so energetically from the inside, instead of trying futilely to control events outside of you.

No matter how you identify by gender, divine forms of both masculine and feminine energy make their way through you at different levels. This list of everyday concepts demonstrates how the two energies can be broadly categorized to serve as examples for your own inner balance and the necessity of both to flow freely:

Yin (Feminine) Energy

Cold

Shade, moon, night

Contemplation, listening, emotional healing

Rest, sleep

Fall, winter

Receiving, incubation

Yang (Masculine) Energy

Heat

Light, sun, day

Action, speaking, physical repairs, movement

Wakefulness

Spring, summer

Giving, producing

As you can see, these complementary expressions of energy rely on each other, coexist in perfect harmony, and "become" each other in cycles and turns, with time or varying attention.

Culturally, most of us in the Western capitalist world are accustomed to greater attention and reward for concepts living in the masculine category. We've been taught over centuries by example and dogma to favor them to the point of toxic patterns showing up in both categories. Although your spiritual power is about developing the self, it will also be very helpful to your personal journey to be able to recognize the effects that the broader culture's imbalance has had on you.

Reflecting back on the last chapter's creative representation of your life's phases, see if you can identify how feminine and masculine energy have played different roles through you and consider how your inner balance of the two has varied for the purpose of different stages.

When I was very young and in confused denial that muffled my full spiritual gifts, one dominant prayer I held in my heart was "God, please use me." At that stage I had picked up a belief that the only appropriate use to be in the world was action-oriented service, so I worked hard to actively help the divine use me through masculine energy instead of cultivating my potential for feeling, listening, and receiving guidance. My many years in professional roles trying to "heal the world" through action were certainly not wasted, but they did also coincide with devastating physical illness and relationship traumas that demanded I ask new questions about my inner balance and take new leaps with my life.

Your own practice and contemplation of your energetic balance may also shine a light where you don't expect it's needed. Have patience with yourself and the process. It won't happen right away or be complete in just a week or a month, but it will be well worth the exploration.

Bob's Story: The Power of Conversation

After I'd been working almost entirely on my own doing spirit readings and workshops for a number of years, one of my longtime threads of connection to nonprofit work with youth who are disadvantaged and at risk started to pull and tug at me again, and it led me to meet Bob Bates. I was visiting the gorgeous Downtown LA campus of Inner-City Arts, a thirty-five-year-old arts organization serving kids living in and around Skid Row. Creative, dynamic young teaching artists and mover-shaker executives mingled in the studios and courtyards that day at an event to support and help relaunch in-person arts programs for youth after the pandemic had tamped everything down for two years. Standing quietly under a sycamore tree was an elderly gentleman with a peaceful smile who seemed to be observing the hustle LA does so well. As soon as speeches began for the event, he was welcomed forward and introduced as the cofounder and artistic director of the whole place.

Over the course of that day and in many conversations I got to have with him later, I learned Bob's story of how this incredible art school full of state-of-the-art equipment, abundant supplies, and passionate, talented teachers came to empower creativity for more than five thousand Los Angeles kids each year. As Bob tells it, it started when he was a young struggling artist and newlywed, and he heard a voice from the mystery of the universe.

"It said, 'You need to get an art space for kids,'" Bob explains.

He was and still is a self-proclaimed "good Christian," and he had learned to meditate (he was also a product of the Los Angeles art community in the 1970s, after all), which helped him cope early on with the natural anxieties of his tenuous career and lack of future plans. He remembers looking up at the high ceiling of the art studio where he'd been working and asking the divine force he knows as God, "Is this it? Is there anything else for me?"

And God, or the great mystery of life itself, as Bob also describes it, responded in conversation. Bob didn't act on what he heard right away, but he continually pondered it and occasionally noticed unmistakable signs urging him forward. A big pallet of paint tubes he hadn't ordered showed up in the middle of the rec room in a community center where he'd been volunteering with children. He found an envelope propped against his door with the details of a grant proposal opportunity to fund a project for youth. And ultimately, another reminder came in conversation, this time through a dream.

Bob says in the dream he was surrounded by a presence that took the shapes of five people, encircling him closely and pointing directly at him. "They said, 'Bob, we've given you five years. If you don't take this assignment, we'll give it to someone else. It's time for this school to become a reality on Planet Earth.'"

Each time he tells the story in conversation with colleagues, visitors, or old friends, Bob emphasizes that part: the messengers he dreamed about insisted specifically that the space to teach art was needed "on Planet Earth." I'm impressed by his boldness when he recounts the details with no apparent concern that people will question the validity of the spirit messages or ridicule his earnest belief that the great mystery of life is actively engaged and directly conversing with us to shape a better world. I met and got to know Bob not too long before it was time for me to launch into writing this book, and in every corner of myself I was so grateful for the conversation.

How Real Change Happens

In a word . . . perfectly. Just as we can have faith in the complementary invisible forces that grow a seed into a tree or make a storm system give way to clear skies, the mechanisms for change in our lives are reliable while remaining somewhat mysterious in process and timing. Sometimes you will receive a distinct message through the spiritual tools you've developed, feel confident in taking a new action because of it, and see a new result in steady succession. Far more often, though, progress is nonlinear and seems badly timed until we look back and realize how many added benefits we gained from the twists, turns, and waiting.

Once you have made a decision to let spirit take its full natural role in your life and choices, remembering the perfection of divine nature will help ease doubt along the way. One of the biggest gifts of your balanced body-mind-spirit apparatus is the wonder and surprise that divine energy brings when you've cleared a path for it to flow through you. That clearing and balancing of our energy is our most important work; more influential than most actions we've taken in the past to manipulate our lives into place.

As you proceed in your newfound relationship with spirit energy, remember that you are the physical mouthpiece for spirit. If there is only one piece of Bob's fantastic story that inspires you to make a change in the way you bring your gifts to the world, I hope it's the speaking up for the divine with confidence part. I'm not talking about evangelizing, trying to convince other people to see the divine the way you do. I mean taking the signals the divine gives you and turning them into a new way of speaking to others from an outlook of possibility, creation, new ideas, and solutions. The universe is calling out as clearly as it can for more voices like that.

For many of us, it feels like a bold choice and takes effort at first to speak and act in new ways that others who may not have tuned in to divine energy will see. Know that you always have companionship for those moments of doubt, and for the wonder and delight waiting for you on the other side. All the support you'll need to overcome those challenging moments is available to you, both in spirit form and through the global community of other divinely engaged souls I can promise you is growing steadily every day.

May the learning experience continue for you every day, always bringing you closer to your own divine nature—and awesome power— during your lifetime!

12

What the World Needs Now: Your Divine Role in Global Change

I promised we'd begin and end with the physical living of our lives because, well, that's the point of being here, even while we're growing our senses for nonphysical spirit energy. The body is what makes us human rather than purely divine, so we'll continually return our focus to the bodily experience until it's time to enter the state our pals and guides in spirit are enjoying. So what are you going to do with your time now that you're ready to engage the fuller scope of your body-mind-spirit self in it? When I work in one-on-one sessions with people asking that question, I'm able to give some specific direction in detail, but here let me at least offer you a directional sign. You decide whether you'd like to follow it.

My Story: The Power of Compassion

Early in my reawakening to the spiritual abilities that I'd been carrying around—like going through a backpack I'd forgotten I'd been wearing and finding it full of supplies to make the most arduous hike glide by smoothly—I learned from a mentor to choose some music that stirred my soul whenever I heard it and make myself a little playlist as I prepared for client readings. I love how that practice, which I still follow so many years later, puts me in odd company with a heavyweight champ striding through the crowd at a boxing match or a baseball player getting pumped up by their walkout song into the batter's box. The endeavors we're each engaged in in those moments have almost nothing to do with each other on the surface, but I am convinced we're all trying to ride our music into the same stream. It's the synchronized flow of body, mind, and spirit that makes us most effective in anything we care most about doing well. The element I need in my playlist that may or may not be essential in an athlete's galvanizing songs, though, is a distinct quality of the divine that I can be sure will call up the same aspect of my inner being to participate front and center in a productive reading. I couldn't define specifically what that quality was until one of my beloved guides showed me so artfully that I couldn't miss or forget it.

The piece of music I first gravitated to for my playlist before a spirit reading was the soaring, united voices in the American composer Morten Lauridsen's requiem, "Lux Aeterna," especially the opening Latin message: *Requiem aeternam dona eis, Domine; et lux perpetua luceat eis* ("Give them eternal rest, O Lord; and let light perpetual shine upon them"). The notes and poetic language instantly call up my sense of reverence along with a visceral feeling of closeness to all those who have died. Even while trusting the process, I'd wonder vaguely: How is it that I can feel so intimately close to a vast and shapeless mass of souls I never met?

The answer came from a cherished friend, Michael, who left his physical body years ago but continues to turn my head when I need to look at things from a new angle or to gain deeper awareness of a spiritual truth.

He helped me recognize the specific, consistent attribute that's aimed at and through us from the realm of divine energy one day when I was listening to the "Lux Aeterna." I'd become instantly aware of Michael's presence when the choir sang its first line. There was some logic to his appearance, since the music comes from a traditional Catholic or Anglican order of honoring the dead that I'd heard many versions of as the kid of choral singers. Michael had been a member of the choir my parents sang in for decades, which had been by extension one of my formative spiritual "neighborhoods." On this memorable day, Michael was there with me, warm as sunshine with a happy laugh that resonated for me soundlessly, to tell me something about the human voices of the "Lux Aeterna," which were ostensibly sending the musical message toward heaven and the spirits of the dead as they'd recorded it. When they sang the prayer for God to grant eternal rest for and let perpetual light shine on the dead, Michael showed me another way to understand it.

"If only they knew," he said as if he were sitting right next to me, "*we* are in there. We're singing these words right back to *them*."

And then I could hear the music I'd heard countless times before transform into something new all at once. While we are worrying about the well-being of the dead, Michael showed me, *the dead* or, more precisely, the eternal souls of all those who have lived before, are intently focused on channeling peace and light toward us as we struggle through the endeavor of living now. The most memorable primary quality I could feel pouring through the music and lyrics? A tsunami of compassion. The divine energy of the universe was singing for *our* well-being with a voice utterly free from worry and full of pure delight at our brave existence.

By that point on my journey I was well conditioned to watch for the ways spirit can flip life upside down and thrill us by surprise. But the message from Michael that day gave me an extra jolt and still does. The possibility he helped me glimpse of our utter peace after death could chip away at some of our biggest human fears and plant a seed of understanding that the supposed ending in death could truly be just a release into an alternate viewpoint toward life. As Helen Keller said, "Death is no more than passing from one room into another."

In the other room, from what I hear from spirits over and over in my readings, a whole lot of compassionate conspiracy seems to be going on.

So What's It Got to Do with Us?

As you incorporate an intentional connection to spirit into your daily life, you'll notice material side effects that you might not have expected, such as inclinations to spend time with different people, speak differently, and take care of yourself in new ways. I mentioned in the book's introduction that you'd get more than just tips for talking to the dead here, because experience has shown me that the skill of mediumship is just a conduit for something more important. Those "side effects" of growing your spirit senses are hints toward the main event. In fostering psychic gifts, we've actually been cultivating a major life change that comes with the real, lived expansion of our day-to-day power. That big news I got about compassion being the primary trait of divine spirit is part of the package. Welcomed in automatically when we connect to spirit with equanimity, the spirit urges us toward a new path we didn't necessarily know we were looking to take.

Compassion is the directional sign I offered earlier to help guide you toward divine perspective on your road ahead, but in all honesty, I'm not sure there's as much of a choice about whether to follow it as I suggested.

Not because of possible judgment from me or a deity or your mother if you don't, but because of the compelling nudges that will come from within you. The body-mind-spirit apparatus we've been balancing and fine-tuning helps make our choices clearer because it's so effective at signaling to us when we're blocking compassionate divine energy flow. Such signals can be a quiet internal revolt, like I felt growing against the aggressive medical interventions to treat my lupus symptoms back in the day, or we might see a more blatant crumbling of a relationship, job, or other situation after we've ignored the quiet inner inklings of compassion for ourselves or others long enough.

Our apparatus also won't let us float around on an ethereal cloud of purely spiritual bliss for very long, as healing and empowering as that respite might be for a time. Our full complement of human senses eventually urges us back into the fray to be part of the natural cycle of life's evolution: conflict, healing, expansion, conflict, healing, and expansion. The Dalai Lama has talked about that phenomenon, saying: "Every day, as soon as I wake up, I meditate on compassion, and it brings me peace and tranquility. It's not just a matter of being free from disturbance, but of being moved by love and compassion. Peace of mind isn't just a religious topic; it underpins the survival of humanity. Even those who trouble us are human beings and deserve our compassion."[18]

Could he be saying the compulsion to act on behalf of divine compassion is part of the deal when we connect to our spiritual essence? That notion might explain why we so often see the most devoted spiritual seekers engaging with the toughest challenges and populations on the edges of society, putting an egocentric life aside to engage actively in compassion

18 "His Holiness the Dalai Lama Speaks on Compassion and Dignity in Schools," Central Tibetan Administration, October 26, 2021, https://tibet.net/his-holiness-the-dalai-lama-speaks-on-compassion-and-dignity-in-schools/.

as their vocation. Examples of that phenomenon stretch far beyond the Dalai Lama's spiritual center and have more of an outward rippling positive impact than is often attributed to the act. I've seen this kind of rippling positive impact in many of the outreach projects I've participated in or consulted on, seeing people of some privilege and resources go in with an altruistic idea of giving to others in need only to see the healing effects resonate back through their own lives. The creative people I've known who volunteer to teach poetry, dance, or gardening to incarcerated individuals always find their own souls fed and uplifted through the interaction, an outcome they rarely had imagined would result from their service to others.

Don't worry. I haven't lured you here to trick you into giving all your energy and resources to the less fortunate or ditching your splashy career for a humble path to heal the world. Your unique body-mind-spirit apparatus can tell you whether you're well suited to either of those shifts over time. The universe clearly values our diverse qualities, which show up in any number of manifestations neither you nor I might imagine. Why else would evolution have led to more than 500 different and strange species of sharks[19] or 7,168 unique human languages?[20] Remember those factoids whenever you catch yourself pushing your child to take up your own favorite pastime or shaking your head at another culture's habits. Our diversity is in our nature for good. Most of all, remember that trying to squeeze everyone into the same uniform is futile. Divine spirit energy points toward some form of compassion in every case but has never, in my countless readings, conveyed a message promoting conformity for conformity's sake.

19 The Ocean Portal Team, "Sharks." Reviewed by David Shiffman for the Smithsonian Institute, April 2018, https://ocean.si.edu/ocean-life/sharks-rays/sharks#:~:text=500%2B%20Species,-Sharks%20come%20in&text=With%20over%20500%20species%20of,39%20feet%20(12%20meters).
20 "How many languages are there in the world?" Ethnologue, SIL Institute, 2023, https://www.ethnologue.com/insights/how-many-languages/.

Just as with career and life choices, I also don't intend to advocate political positions here, although anyone in a Western military-industrial powerhouse country like mine knows the tendency for compassion to become a political topic. As a young idealist in college, I even chose to major in Politics and Public Policy Analysis, thinking that was the best route to contributing to a positive impact on humanity someday. But in the course of my "independent study" of spirit, I discovered politics wouldn't be the place for me to channel my specific abilities. Yes, the government and institutions of our countries have a powerful role in the people's quality of life, and we could use a lot more divinely attuned participants in them. But some of our globe's biggest dangers need more than that to change. The anti-compassionate scourges of racism, sexism, classism, and nationalism—and some of their kin, such as mass incarceration, economic disparity, mental health crises, violence, child hunger, environmental destruction, and warfare profiteering to name a few—become intractable as long as we leave them solely to the political realm for endless debate. While I won't tell you what to think or how and whether to act on any of the issues themselves, I believe the collective spiritual attunement of citizens and leaders alike will naturally bring divine well-being into more corners of society.

Instead of dictating your path, I hope to encourage you forward on any road designated by that directional sign "compassion." That guidance allows you to wander away from political influence and apart from societal expectations onto less congested routes where peace, tranquility, and kindness prevail above all else. Discover how you move, speak, and relate to others and how you feel within yourself as you travel them. Your choice to read this book tells me you've likely danced on some of those roads enough to recognize a lot of their features, and yet the state of the world tells me all of us could use a boost now and then to help us stick with them for more transformative effects to spread and take hold.

TRY THIS: I'll call this exercise the three-week compassion reboot. Throughout the book, I've contended that your essential nature is divine, and now I'm adding that the trait that drives the divine is compassion. So why aren't all humans constantly compassionate with each other? Some religious leaders might jump in here and veer us onto a tangent about original sin, and celebrated philosophers have their own ideas about morality and the lack of it. In my approach, I try my best to leave room for plenty of diverse theories while getting practical about living your best day-to-day life. This tool recognizes the scientific principle that our participation in the collective energy of the globe is fundamental to life— meaning we are, at our most fundamental physical existence, energy, and we constantly exchange energy with the energy of our surroundings. Over these three weeks, we're going to help shape experience (the body's role) and thought (the mind's role) to empower the spirit to play its destined role of compassionate conspiracy.

The first week is to detox, which you can think of as a time to focus on the energy you're asking your physical apparatus to cope with internally and externally. Remember the tips in Chapter 1 about the quality of food and other ingestibles you choose, the environments you physically immerse yourself in (like my client Clara's gravitation toward saltwater), and the general quality of the company you keep, including your engagement with information and people remotely. When I work with a client for whom the world's woes have become a painful fixation, often manifested as "doomscrolling" online to constantly seek and engage with negative or depressing information, I know there is no instant solution. But we can start with this week of intentional awareness and the continual choice to detox the body of such energy. As you try it, be honest with yourself about what you know you need to avoid—there is no reason to declare to anyone else that you're on a program or that you're "being good" during this week. Your body-mind-spirit apparatus will be your judge.

In week two, you'll start to reboot your system with an infusion of compassion-rich thinking. And oooo-eeee, this step is not easy for a lot of us. As early as young childhood, we start to hold grudges for minor playground offenses. By adulthood, most of us have suffered more egregious treatment by both intimates and strangers. We cannot snap our fingers to feel forgiving, compassionate energy about them or the circumstances their actions fueled. The key to this week's thought experiment is to slowly train your mind to evaluate those people and circumstances from a more casual observer's view, where forgiveness and compassion have an easier way in. (This is a good time to bring out your journal again to write your new observations down.) For a few minutes each day, choose a personal, social, or global offense you've experienced and think of the person or people behind it from a neutral description of their motivations, the likely sources of their beliefs, and the possible experience they had (or continue to have) as the perpetrator of hurtful acts. That's it. Fill your thoughts and journal with this specific empathy, and see what happens. Research suggests that your ability to shift toward a forgiving view not only has mental health benefits but improves physical well-being too.[21] Look at that! A two-for-one deal for your body and mind.

Finally in week three, your compassion reboot makes way for your spirit to take a more naturally active role, through inspiration of

21 Catherine Pearson, "The Emotional Relief of Forgiving Someone." "Well" (newsletter), *New York Times*, updated May 1, 2023, https://www.nytimes.com/2023/04/28/well/forgive-ness-mental-health.html?smid=nytcore-ios-share&referringSource=articleShare&fbclid=I-wAR2KxDM5DJbBB23u9Xv2XsinEkg87Oxq7r9Hhiy7KeIw9py8TiZer9QB1U.

new experience. Ideally this new state you've cultivated will go on and on uninterrupted, but for this one week, simply make a point of noticing and affirming in writing what is happening. What are you suddenly drawn to try that you would have never pursued before? Are you speaking up differently in meetings or in conversations with friends and family than your old norms allowed? Celebrate in your journal the small and big ways your life is starting to prove you've empowered divine energy to flow freely and actively.

Here are some changes you can watch for when your body-mind-spirit being has rebooted to fixate on the power of goodness and compassion to grow instead of on the frustration or pain from your surroundings. You see new outlets, you hear better news, and you meet new allies. Especially in that new communion with other people who are also fixating *their* souls on a peaceful and loving universe, you notice visible progress in your work and social environments starts to happen faster. I've certainly seen it in every area of my life by adhering to my one nonnegotiable, daily job requirement: to orient and reorient myself as often as needed to align with the divine perspective of compassion.

You're Not on Your Own from Here

Whatever confusion you may be left with after converting the ideas and experiences in this book into your own approach, please know you have plenty of good company as you engage the ongoing mysteries. None of us reaches a pinnacle of peace and wisdom and stays there for very long at one stretch. My ultimately realized identity as a mystic is entirely centered on the unknown. The concept that I've finally internalized is rooted in the early meaning of the word mystic, which comes from the Old French *mistique*, meaning "mysterious or full of mystery," and came to mean "spiritually allegorical, pertaining to mysteries of faith" in the late fourteenth century. I experience my path and work as a constant search for the hidden truths of our lives. It does take some practice, but if you can get comfy with a state of not knowing, it turns out some incredible secret doors, which seem to open up to you like magic.

Through each passage, figurative and literal, that I've crossed on the journey with spirit, I've found some new invigorating connection or companionship I didn't have before. Considering the last fifty years saw rates of loneliness double among adults in the United States, I wish more people knew that the tools for perpetual spiritual connection have been right there in their backpack all along.[22]

If solitary activities like meditation and solo prayer have formed your notion of spiritual life until now, get ready for your everyday experience of mingling and collaborating with others to take on spiritual significance. People's purpose and vocation don't need to look a thing like my mystical life for them to be fully engaged with divine spirit power in what they do, either. Let the stories I've shared about clients, friends, and mentors remind you of the innumerable faces of body-mind-spirit alignment moving through your life. Antonio, Melissa, Cadence, Rob, Jamie, Clara, Monica, Don, Elaine, Alicia, Bob, Hannah, Rick—not one of them holds a job with a hint of the "woo-woo" or a mystical label. Yet every one of them is making powerful, world-improving use of their time here. In Rick's case, although he was once a church minister, I think he might agree that his direct relationship with divine spirit energy—my words, not his—has grown much richer and deeper since he left that official role. There is no prescription or mapped route for you to follow now, but you have what you need for the road.

---

22 Shainna Ali, "What You Need to Know About the Loneliness Epidemic." *Psychology Today*, July 12, 2018, https://www.psychologytoday.com/us/blog/modern-mentality/201807/ what-you-need-know-about-the-loneliness-epidemic.

You're ready to test your senses and try some alternate routes with plenty of company and those well-tended body-mind-spirit tools as guidance.

Oh, And One More Thing

A note on testing out new tools. In any field, using new tools, whether they're tools you hold in your hands or something more metaphorical, won't be all smooth success and glory, no matter what lucky beginners say. When you go back to any of the "try this" exercises I've shared or when you set off on a new adventure to see how you manage entirely on your own instincts, it will help to think of yourself as an artist—or artisan, even better—of your own life experience, including its successes and apparent failures. I distinguish between those two creative labels here because to me "artisan" suggests a perpetual honing of a craft until something both beautiful and usable, both functional and unique takes shape. I want you to have the same delight that the divine takes from seeing your life take shape beautifully, errors and all.

Not long ago, I decided to give the social media platform TikTok a try to check out my assumption that its content was all trivial, fame-seeking nonsense. The diversity of videos and content creators I found proved that reputation wrong, and I've especially loved the myriad artists, champions of the environment, educators, and voices of indigenous wisdom from around the world populating my feed. Recently I watched, enthralled, while a woodworker from Georgia named Jeb Redwine (now there's a mystical name!) shared his first meticulous attempt at making a decorative copper belt buckle and narrated the whole experiment with light candor. At one point in the video, he realized he'd have to toss out all of his work on his first, time-consuming attempt at making the buckle he'd envisioned, sketched, cut, and drilled, using up materials along the way.

"While at times soul-crushing, I believe failure is an incredibly valuable source of instruction," Jeb's boyish, country voice says as we see him wiping everything off his workbench for a fresh start. "Acquiring any degree of proficiency at anything takes hours of practice and the tenacity to overcome countless mistakes. So if you're gonna fail, you might as well fail big, as I have with this project, and try to learn as much as you can from the process."[23]

The quiet, matter-of-fact, and humble tone of his words struck me with bright, powerful clarity, which is one of my favorite ways divine spirit shows up any and every day. This artisan Jeb Redwine, whom I may never encounter in person, spoke to my soul with an offering I knew both you and I needed, at just the right time.

When a face in a crowd, a line in a book, or a sentence from a stranger lights up with a unique, bright clarity you just can't shake, listen to the quiet voice urging you to heed it. And let that spirit of craftsmanship, with all its adventurous, forgiving, challenging delight, course through your life.

---

23 Redwinewooddesign, TikTok video, https://www.tiktok.com/@redwinewooddesign/video/7224208989662317866?is_from_webapp=1.

Acknowledgments

A finished book is another bit of physical evidence of the divine energy flowing through many souls. I could accomplish my part of the job only because of the continuous support, thoughtful advice, immense talent, proactive love, physical effort, direct challenges, and clear instructions of more people (and some animal friends) than I could possibly name here. Thank you, everyone. I'm blessed by the serendipity of our lives intersecting.

To the tiny miracles who grew me up fast and then grew yourselves up into my favorite, very tall, very funny company—Anabel, Mason, and August—you three literally are God's gift to the world, as humble as you are and as biased as I might be. Thank you for your patience and strength to your core during the hard parts and your silliness and creativity always. The circle of family around us, radiating out in ring after ring of remarkable relatives, has propped, prodded, and propelled us without pause. Mom and Pa, Alison and Dan, Susannah and Zach, and all the dogs from Sheba on, you've been the perfect nest. And to all my grandparents, aunts, uncles, and cousins, whether great-great or once or twice removed, you've enriched my spiritual heritage and set enough different examples of divine love for me to study over many lifetimes.

All the teachers I've had, whether professional or accidental, have demonstrated to me the truth that utter reverence can be aptly drawn from and applied to any subject in the universe. The ones I encountered early who still stand out in my mind and daily application of their lessons—including Joan Wagner, Corky Lemon, Merrill Bolster, Genevieve Miller, Vicki Bush, Rick Adams, John Thomas, Graciela Kaplan, Carmie Rodriguez, Greg Feldmeth, Alan Geier, Susan Grether, Mike Babcock, Stan Sheinkopf, Chuck Ellis, Fred Sontag, David Menefee-Libey, and Lorn Foster—impressed upon me the divine traits of patience, curiosity, diligence, precision, physical and intellectual rigor, humor, and kindness as they practiced instead of preaching them. Those essential role models prepared me to hear the mentors, teachers, and activists who later helped ground, shape, and expand my spiritual identity into daily practice: George Regas, Tim Safford, Ed Bacon, Desmond Tutu, Zelda Kennedy, Gary Hall, Rick Thyne, Jesse Jackson, Bryan Stevenson, Greg Boyle, Marian Wright Edelman, Fleur Leussink, Andrew Huskey, and all of the courageous clients who've opened up to spirit readings, Reiki healing, and workshops with me over the years. You've all made "lifelong student" into my most beloved vocation.

Though completing this first book nearly flattened me once or twice, I'm starting to think "author" might be a new favorite vocation. Thank you to everyone at Apollo for supporting that reality, especially Julia Abramoff, Adam O'Brien, and Drew Anderla for your caring and meticulous attention to my work. I'd like to shout praise far and wide to all the writers who've stirred my passion for language and living singularly as a body-mind-spirit, like Isabel Allende, Barbara Kingsolver, Tom Robbins, Ross Gay, Gabriel

García Márquez, Mary Oliver, Pablo Neruda, Toni Morrison, Anne Lamott, Joy Harjo, Mary Karr, Lydia Davis, bell hooks, Patti Smith, Mark Salzman, Susie Petruccelli, and Gillian Kessler. The last two are precious childhood friends who each boldly put their hearts and words into book form, then boosted my bravery and freely shared hard-earned lessons to ease my way. Cadence Petros, Marya Gould, and Monica Bencze, I can't imagine tackling this hill without you either; I thank you for continually giving of yourselves with total abandon. Magically, you keep becoming even more glorious selves too.

As Snoop Dogg said upon receiving his star on the Hollywood Walk of Fame, "Last but not least, I wanna thank me. I wanna thank me for believing in me." He went on to elaborate quite a bit, but for me and my higher spirit self perpetually calling me forward, that much will do for now.